SCHOOLS MUST SPEAK FOR THEMSELVES

Schools must speak for themselves. In a political and economic climate in which school performance is made public, performance tables and inspectors' reports can only tell a partial story. Sometimes they get it wrong.

Self-critical and self-confident schools are information rich. They know how to tell their story for themselves and they welcome the external account as another source of evidence, another view on policy and practice.

This book illustrates how schools can tell their own story. It draws on ground-breaking work with the National Union of Teachers to demonstrate a practical approach to identifying what makes a good school and the part that pupils, parents and teachers can play in school improvement. Its usefulness to, and use by, classroom teachers will prove to be its greatest strength in an ever-expanding effectiveness literature.

John MacBeath is Professor of Education and Director of the Quality in Education Centre at the University of Strathclyde. He works with British and International governments in an advisory capacity, and is a key figure in the debate surrounding standards in education.

SCHOOLS MUST SPEAK FOR THEMSELVES

The case for school self-evaluation

John MacBeath

London and New York

First published 1999
by Routledge
11 New Fetter Lane, London EC4P 4EE

Simultaneously published in the USA and Canada
by Routledge
29 West 35th Street, New York, NY 10001

Typeset in Palatino by RefineCatch Limited, Bungay, Suffolk
Printed and bound in Great Britain by
TJ International Ltd, Padstow, Cornwall

British Library Cataloguing in Publication Data
A catalogue record for this book is available from the British Library

Library of Congress Cataloging in Publication Data
MacBeath, John E. C.
Schools must speak for themselves: the case for school self-evaluation /
John MacBeath and the NUT.
p.   cm.
Includes bibliographical references (p.   ) and index.
1. Educational evaluation – Great Britain.   2. Schools – Great
Britain – Evaluation.   3. Educational change – Great Britain.
I. National Union of Teachers.   II. Title.
LB2822.75.M33   1999   98–31538
CIP

ISBN 0–415–20580–8

CONTENTS

ILLUSTRATIONS

DIAGRAMS

TABLES

FOREWORD

In 1995 the National Union of Teachers commissioned a study of school self-evaluation. Its purpose was to discover if the kind of model that had been developed in Scotland in the early 1990s could be applied or redeveloped in an English/Welsh context. The resulting publication, 'Schools Speak for Themselves' (SSFT as it is widely referred to), was launched in January 1996 and sent by the NUT to every primary, secondary and special school in England and Wales. Further copies were ordered by authorities, universities and libraries, and by early 1998 the supply had been exhausted. The decision to republish was, however, over-taken by events. Much had happened in the intervening three years, not least a change of government, and it seemed like a good idea to find out what had happened to SSFT in the intervening period. Was it still relevant? Or, for that matter, had it ever been relevant? And, if so, for whom?

In the summer of 1998 the NUT commissioned a follow-up study to answer these questions. What had people actually done with the original? Had they read it? Had they used it? Or had it been hidden in a dark cupboard? Had it had an impact on policy or practice? And, if so, at what level and with what implications for teachers, headteachers, parents or pupils? Some of the findings from that study are included in this volume.

Schools Must Speak for Themselves is a revisiting of the original study, updating it, drawing on uses made of it by schools and authorities to suggest practical ways in which it might be used and developed. The book is in four parts. The first section puts the case for self-evaluation and reviews the research which has made such a contribution to our thinking about effective and improving schools. The second section describes the original study, including some revisions of the original text. The third section examines the follow-up at school and authority level and compares the SSFT approach with what happens in other countries. The fourth section describes the key aspects of a framework for self-evaluation and provides a step-by-step guide to the SSFT process. A final concluding chapter summarises the findings and examines implications for wider policy-making.

ACKNOWLEDGEMENTS

My first thanks are to the many people in the National Union of Teachers who have underwritten this work from the outset; to Doug McAvoy for his continuing and total support for the Schools Speak for Themselves project, which has helped to give it such a high profile nationally. A particular vote of thanks to John Bangs, who had a good idea in the first place, who pursued it and, three years after our first meeting, is still giving me the benefit of his astute insights and prescient judgement. Neither the 1995 nor the 1999 publication would have been the same without his thoughtful contribution.

Three people worked with me on the 1995 study, visiting schools, gathering data, acting as critical friends and fulfilling that role in a way that generated a great deal of insightful comment from pupils, parents and teachers. To Brian Boyd, Jim Rand and Steve Bell, sincere thanks for exemplifying the role of the critical friend so effectively and for their contributions to the original publication. And to Charles Howie, who did most of the legwork for the 1999 follow-up study.

A thank-you to the ten schools who were involved in the 1995 study and to the many teachers, headteachers and authorities who contributed to the follow-up study. One of the heads from the original study, Anne Waterhouse, is now an authority adviser but continues to promote SSFT and has written an account of her experiences for this book. I have learned a great deal from her.

Three other people also wrote, eloquently, about their involvement with SSFT – Roger Edwardson, James Learmonth and Leif Moos. All three have been more than contributors. They have become valued colleagues and personal friends.

My gratitude to Lorne Gregg for the many, and sometimes tedious, hours in editing and formatting the text, and to Sandra MacBeath for her careful reading of the manuscript, for the endless drafting and redrafting and critical comment where it was deserved. My thanks also go to the University of Strathclyde who supported and endorsed our work.

Finally to Nina Stibbe of Routledge, who had faith in the book from the word go and by her enthusiasm persuaded Arthur Jarman and John Bangs of the NUT that schools would speak for themselves, with Routledge's help.

1

WHY SCHOOLS MUST SPEAK FOR THEMSELVES

Schools speak for themselves. They sometimes do so unconsciously, conveying implicit messages about their priorities and values. Some schools are able to speak for themselves with a high degree of self-awareness and self-assurance. They know their strengths and are secure enough to acknowledge their weaknesses.

It is an index of a nation's educational health when its school communities have a high level of intelligence and know how to use the tools of self-evaluation and self-improvement. In healthy systems there is sharing and networking of good practice within and among schools on a collegial basis. It is an unhealthy system which relies on the constant routine attentions of an external body to police its schools.

Evaluating the role of the external inspection, Roger Frost HMI quotes Denis Healey's autobiography: 'What you do not know, indeed what you cannot know, is often more important than what you do know. The darkness does not destroy what it conceals.'[1]

Canadian researchers[2] found that classroom observations by visiting auditors fail to touch the real day-to-day experiences of children and their teachers. In one school in our 1995 study students warned us to be wary of using impressions of visitors as a source of evidence. They said they had become very well trained on how to show the school off to its best for outsiders and inspectors. One student described the school as 'a Jekyll and Hyde school with two faces. It has one face for visitors and one for us.'

There is an emerging consensus and body of wisdom about what a healthy system of school evaluation looks like. Its primary goal is to help schools to maintain and improve through critical self-reflection. It is concerned to equip teachers with the know-how to evaluate the quality of learning in their classrooms so that they do not have to rely on an external view, yet welcome such a perspective because it can enhance and strengthen good practice.

In such a system there is an important role for an Inspectorate or Office of Standards: to make itself as redundant as possible. It does so by seeking to reinforce the foundations of self-review and by helping schools to build more effectively on those foundations. HMI in Wales, Scotland and Northern Ireland and OFSTED in England are charged with monitoring and reporting to ministers and the secretary of state on standards in the nation's schools, but that is not their only, or even their primary, role. Their primary role is to help to *raise* standards, a goal that can be achieved first and foremost by helping schools to know themselves, do it for themselves and to give their own account of their achievements.

Who tells your story? This is the question put to schools by ex-HMI David Green in his work with Chicago schools.[3] Is it the council or the local authority? Is it the test-makers and the assessment industry? Is it the politicians? Is it the local or national press? Is it Hollywood with its mythic classrooms (*Blackboard Jungle, Dangerous Minds, Dead Poets Society, Mr Holland's Opus*)? David Green describes being met at the airport by an inspector whose licence plate bore the letters 'I EVALUATE'. Often it is others who claim the right to speak on behalf of schools, to tell their stories for them, to amend and abridge and to add their own ending.

The 'story' is powerful because it is crucial to recognise that schools have a history, a unique cast of characters and a narrative that unfolds over time in unanticipated directions. That is how evaluation works – a continuing and continually revealing process. This is where school improvement takes root.

Diagram 1.1, adapted from school improvement work by Michael Schratz and his colleagues in Austria, describes three dimensions of school evaluation and development.[4] The internal–external dimension represents a continuum from self-evaluation to evaluation from an outside source. Some systems could be depicted as lying at the extreme external end – that is, where the monitoring of quality and standards rests solely with an external inspectorate. In some systems there is no external body and quality assurance is exclusively the province of the school itself. Somewhere between is the point of balance of the two. Where this balance lies will differ from one country to another, and from one context to another but finding it is critical to the pursuit of quality and standards.

The pressure-support axis describes a continuum with, at one end, a high level of support from 'the system' and at the other extremity strong pressure. While this dimension is very real and highly significant, it is mainly in a subjective sense. That is, pressure and support are best understood in terms of what people experience, whether or not they feel that they are under pressure or whether they feel supported. Again there is a point of balance and it can only be found when there is a feedback loop which takes account of people's individual and collective

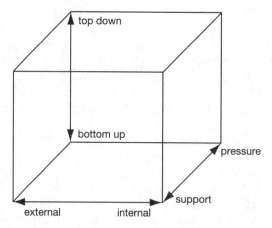

Diagram 1.1 Three dimensions of school evaluation and development

experiences. When that point of balance is achieved, people are enabled to do their job most effectively because they experience intrinsic satisfaction as well as extrinsic recognition and reward. The challenge to improve and to exceed their own expectations then comes primarily from within.

The top-down to bottom-up axis represents how a system sees and implements change. At one extreme it is delivered from above, by dictat, by legislation, by national structures. Alternatively, it can come entirely from below, from class teachers, from pupils and parents, building on day-to-day school and classroom practice. Most commentators agree that neither extreme is ideal and that the best kind of system is one in which bottom-up development is supported and endorsed from the top down.

This is a useful framework for thinking about how schools develop and improve. It is now widely accepted that this works best when there is the optimum blend of all three – support and pressure, bottom-up and top-down change, internal and external evaluation.[5] Achieving the blend is the key factor in determining whether schools will grow and flourish or stagnate and decline. In the best of all possible worlds the direction of change will be from pressure to support, from bottom up to top down and from internal to external evaluation. This optimum blend will, however, differ from area to area and school to school depending on history, context and culture and depending on each school's state of psychological health.

SCHOOLS ARE DIFFERENT

We have seen schools in which self-evaluation could take root and flourish almost overnight. In those schools there was so much energy at teacher and pupil level that pressure and top-down direction would have been counter-productive. We also saw schools in which there was a pervasive cynicism, sometimes at the level of leadership, a climate which dragged teachers down and was damaging to students' motivation and progress. We came across relatively high-achieving schools which were self-satisfied and complacent, limiting opportunities for teachers to grow professionally and inimical to the learning potential of young people. We worked with embattled schools with a reservoir of goodwill but without time, expertise or energy to turn things round. And most typical of all in our experience were the curate's egg schools, good in parts, excellent in other parts, weak in some and with small dark corners into which light rarely seemed to penetrate.

During a recent self-evaluation workshop, a few departmental heads in a secondary school said that they would rather not know how well or badly they were doing either as teachers or as a department. One departmental head said that, as far as he was concerned, ignorance was bliss. 'When ignorance is bliss it is folly to be wise': so went the theme tune of a 1940s radio programme and it is a point of view easier to understand than to condemn. If you have done something badly, or less well than you had hoped, you might prefer not to look at the evaluations. You might wish to spare your ego further distress. As a long-term professional strategy, it is, however, clearly untenable.

So, the optimum balance has to be finely judged depending on the circumstances of the school. That is why the routine OFSTED or OHMCI cycle of inspections is inefficient and ill-informed. It treats schools as if their needs and skills were all the same. It proceeds from a single, simple model, essentially external and top down, the balance of pressure or support dependent on the qualities of any given inspection team.

Those of us who grew up in the fifties and sixties were weaned on a children's literature of public schools, – Enid Blyton, St Trinian's, *Tom Brown's Schooldays*, Ronald Searle. In those fictions, which have, in all probability, shaped the images and values of generations, there were two separate realities – the world of the children and the world of classrooms and 'skool'. There was an implicit assumption that what teachers taught in classrooms was what children learned, and that what went on in the underlife of the school could be put aside when you entered the classroom and got down to real lessons. Yet, with a curious ambivalence, there was also a view that it was on the playing fields and through the ethos of the school's corporate life that character and leadership were forged, and proconsuls prepared for power.

Lindsay Anderson's film *If . . .* was perhaps the first to bring into sharp juxtaposition the two realities of school life and to show that they were, in fact, intrinsically connected. In that film the informal pupil culture breaks through into the formal culture with devastating impact. The film *Kes* did the same work for the comprehensive school. It is, in its way, a classic piece of school evaluation, illuminating the connections between individual learning and school culture, between a bottom-up and top-down perspective on school life.

It was not until the 1970s or so that schools began to treat with serious concern issues of bullying, sexual harassment and racism. Ignorance had hitherto been bliss and it was in some places a matter of policy to turn a blind eye to what went on in the underlife of the school. It is, of course, still characteristic of many institutional cultures, most notably prisons.

Bullying has been exposed through schools' willingness to self-evaluate. Equal opportunities policies have been given shape because the nature of the problem was recognised at a general level and in the specific context of the individual school. It is not school inspectors who can evaluate the extent of bullying in a school nor can they 'inspect in' a solution. It takes all the stakeholders in a school community to recognise and to deal with it. The same holds true for much of what is truly significant in the life of the school – psychological and physical safety, mutual respect, goodwill, motivation, morale, equity, relationships and communication.

Perhaps the most crucial indicator of school quality – how pupils learn – also tends to elude inspection. To know and understand learning requires the studied long-term insights and analysis of teachers and pupils reflecting together, using tools and finding the language to get inside the learning process. The external support and challenge comes from an increasingly rich body of literature on learning derived from painstaking long-term observation and analysis by researchers.

EVALUATION – WITH PURPOSE

Any attempt to evaluate a school or any other organisation is founded on values and purposes, covert or explicit. Over twenty years ago, based on his experience of evaluation in the American school system, Ernest House said:

Contrary to common belief, evaluation is not the ultimate arbiter, delivered from our objectivity and accepted as the final judgement. Evaluation is always derived from biased origins. When someone wants to defend something or to attack something, he often evaluates it. Evaluation is a motivated behaviour. Likewise, the way in which the results of an evaluation are accepted depends on whether they help or hinder the person receiving them. Evaluation is an integral part of the political processes of our society.[6]

THE POLITICAL PURPOSE

Ernest House reminds us that before we embark on discussion of more grandiose purposes we must be alert to political agendas, both on the large, international stage and in the micro-context of school and classroom. Evaluation is motivated behaviour. Its purpose is rarely without prejudice. It does not often set forth simply to 'find out' in a disinterested and speculative way. Evaluation usually comes with a mandate, a price, and with an audience in mind. The audience is crucially important because the language of evaluation has to persuade and convince, however balanced and fair-minded it strives to be.

OFSTED has been quick to recognise the importance of the audience. Which audience is Her Majesty's Chief Inspector most keen to appeal to and why is it important? His primary audience is the public at large, and shaping that constituency is seen as crucial in winning hearts and minds and in securing the ideological high ground. If we have learned one thing in the lifetime of OFSTED, it is its highly political character.

But the same is also increasingly true of schools. Headteachers and teachers in the 1990s are much more likely to see themselves as operating in a political arena than they, or their predecessors, ever did before. The story told publicly about their schools through performance tables is one that they see as, at best, incomplete, at worst 'a tale told by an idiot'. It is therefore incumbent on them to fill out or to retell the story. In modern parlance, it is called 'putting a spin on it' because political spinning is now openly acknowledged as a prerequisite of a free market.

While awareness of the political context of evaluation is crucial for schools and school leadership, it is not a guiding precept. Evaluation has other explicit purposes, often pursued in conjunction with one another. Herein lies the problem. If the purpose of evaluation is not clear and honest in respect of who it is for and who will benefit, it will be attended by confusion and mistrust.

THE ACCOUNTABILITY PURPOSE

One purpose for the story we tell about our schools is to satisfy parents and public that we are not reckless with the money which taxpayers have invested, nor reckless with the lives and futures of children. The story is an 'account' and accountability has a noble purpose. To protect the interests of individuals and of democracy is an inherent requirement of public institutions and a defining characteristic of 'professionalism'.

Accountability has always been implicit and sometimes painfully explicit, as in the system of payment by results of the last century. The 1980s did, however, mark a modern watershed in the place and purpose of accountability. Under the Thatcher regime, the idea of a 'market' in education was born, and the market mechanism was to measure inputs and outputs. Appropriating the language of commerce, its purpose was to evaluate returns on public investment. Auditing was born and school accounts were no longer stories told by people but figures and tables produced by statisticians and bookkeepers. John Gray and Brian Wilcox have this to say about figures: 'To those who would maintain that the figures "speak for themselves" we would merely observe that we have yet to find a single figure that could speak, let alone for itself.'[7]

The authors go on to alert us to the dangers of 'raw' exam or test results for accountability purposes. Used in this way, results 'run the distinct risk of rewarding schools for the "quality" of the intakes they can attract rather than what they actually do for pupils'.[8]

Schools are primarily accountable for what they do for pupils. In order to ascertain what it is they 'do', the primary source of information lies with the accounts of pupils themselves, the quality of their work, and the progress and achievements they make over time. Other sources of knowledge are with those who know and work with pupils in different settings – the two most important sources being teachers and parents.

Schools which speak for themselves account for the trust invested in them by giving quality accounts, providing evidence for what is deemed to be worthwhile and, as schools, how they measure up to that trust.

THE PROFESSIONAL DEVELOPMENT PURPOSE

In the 1960s and 1970s, self-evaluation, like the model of teacher as researcher, stemmed from a notion of the teacher as an 'extended professional'.[9] Evaluation, and self-evaluation in particular, was valued for its contribution to professional growth.

Staff development 'enhances the quality of pupil learning by identifying, clarifying, and meeting the individual needs of the staff within the context of the institution as a whole' writes Eric Hewton.[10] This view of staff development seems no more than common sense but it is a counsel often observed in the breach. Its commonsensical yet counter-intuitive nature is neatly illustrated in Roland Barthes's metaphor of the airline steward's advice to passengers: 'put the oxygen mask on your own face first before putting it on the child's face.'

Without the oxygen of development, without high morale among teachers, how can we expect high morale of children? Without teacher self-esteem and job satisfaction, how could we possibly sustain the self-esteem and satisfaction of pupils?

Teachers are the best judges of their own professional development, although they are not the only judges. Schools, authorities and training providers need systematic data on how teachers view their professional development but this has to be much more than feedback on in-service events. It must essentially be about the school as a place which encourages and sustains professional growth.

THE ORGANISATIONAL DEVELOPMENT PURPOSE

Evaluation involves gathering information to help decision-making. In a school context, therefore, any information or insight which assists the process of decision-making may be regarded as a form of evaluation. The key practical task is to decide what information is needed and how it might be gathered.

Decision-making based on good data is inherently superior to decisions made on the basis of poor data. Informed evaluation helps the organisation itself to become more intelligent. 'The purpose of an organisation is to help ordinary human beings to do extraordinary things' writes Peter Drucker.[11] In other words, the capacity of the individual – the individual pupil or individual teacher – is multiplied when you have a social setting in which people are enabled to learn from one another and, by virtue of the quality of their discourse, to develop a collective intelligence which is greater than the sum of the individuals put together.

If this seems fanciful, consider what can happen in an organisation which lacks those qualities and lacks the capacity to learn from its members. History is littered with examples of organisations which could not learn. Military history offers some of the most tragic examples of decisions taken based on wrong data, not because the data were not available but because people in power chose, for reasons of hierarchy, status and self-interest, to ignore it.[12] The provenance of the information was too low-ranking. 'There are too many cases where organisations know less than their members. There are even cases in which the organisation cannot seem to learn what everybody knows.'[13] Argyris and Schon go on to say that organisational learning 'is the process by which an organisation obtains and uses new knowledge, tools, behaviours and values.' Good tools, as we know from the cave dwellers onwards, extend human intelligence. Smart schools are those which have, and know how to use, simple, economical and routine evaluation tools – shadowing, photographs and videos, spot checks, focus groups, diaries, interviews, feedback boxes, surveys or questionnaires. These are the media through which the intelligence of an organisation – military, business or school – expands and enriches. In David Hargreaves', terms this is where knowledge creation begins.[14]

THE IMPROVEMENT OF TEACHING PURPOSE

Teachers are natural evaluators. The nature and complexity of teaching means that teachers are involved, on a day-to-day basis, in evaluative activities, reviewing their work and the work of their pupils and modifying their practice accordingly. In teaching, as in many other professions, the commitment to critical and systematic reflection on practice is at the heart of what it means to be a 'professional'. It is the basis for individual and collective professional development. Self-evaluation by teachers for teachers is not new and should not be seen as an additional burden.

From their first experience of the 'crit', when college tutors visit to assess their performance, teachers have argued that 'performance' is indeed the most apt description of those often undermining events. The inherent limitations of the one-off evaluation by an external observer are recognised by teachers and pupils alike. This is not to say that we cannot learn a lot from observing what teachers do. In fact, there is a rich and revealing literature on the subject but it is derived from in-depth observation, negotiation and exploration between teacher and observer. The philosopher Ludwig Wittgenstein said that you must cross over a place many times and in different directions before you truly get to know it. That is true of classrooms and the 'performing art' of teaching. Self-evaluation in the classroom has that character. It is an ongoing and in-depth exploration of the art and science of teaching and welcomes the insights that other perspectives can bring.

THE IMPROVEMENT OF LEARNING PURPOSE

Perhaps the two most important purposes of evaluation are to determine what and how pupils are learning and to assess the value of that learning. Evaluating for decision-making, for professional development or for teaching should, in themselves, guarantee a certain quality of learning. However, our experience tells us that this is not necessarily so. We know of children, perhaps our own, who go to good schools in which there are exemplary planning, inspirational leadership and committed teachers but in which they still fail to achieve their potential and are desperately unhappy. Learning has its own life and its own curious logic and illogic.

This is the paradox. It is impossible to teach effectively without a constant stream of feedback about how pupils are learning, yet it is virtually impossible for teachers to deal with the depth and complexity of evaluating the learning of the thirty, one hundred or even two hundred individuals they are required to teach in the course of a week. Much of teaching rests, therefore, on an act of faith that children are learning. The challenge is to develop evaluation systems which relieve teachers of much of the burden of evaluating learning and which put the responsibility into the hands of learners themselves and, wherever appropriate, into the hands of their parents.

It is clear that in the years since our original study for the National Union of Teachers schools are increasingly well informed and creative in their approach to self-evaluation. There are many inventive and interesting approaches being used, to track and monitor achievement and to include the views of stakeholders. But there still does not appear to be much sharing of this expertise, and often outstanding practice, on a wider national basis. That is the challenge to governmental bodies and non-governmental bodies, to unions and teacher education institutions. The commitment to education, education, education carries with it a commitment to learn from the good, from the best, from the ambitious and from the innovators.

This will be realised by putting into the custody of teachers approaches which they can use in their day-to-day practice. Learning and teaching improve when teachers have the tools and grasp the value of being learners in their own class-rooms. Schools improve when they provide opportunities and time for teachers to share with one another. The system as a whole improves when schools are enabled to learn from one another. Governmental decision-making improves when policy-makers listen to teachers and are prepared to learn from them.

2

HUNT THE UNICORN
The search for the effective school

The search for the effective school is like the hunt for the unicorn, a quest for a mythical entity. While few of those who have been involved in the research have believed there existed such a paragon, the term 'the effective school' has nonetheless often been used in the singular, and the notion of 'best' practice often seems to subsume that virtuous state. The inherent problem of the idealised school and the best practice model is expressed by Hampden-Turner and Trompenaars in this way: 'The attempt to avoid conflict, dilemma and ambiguity by putting one's faith in the bottom line, the unicorn's pure and mythic extremity.'[1]

Conflict, dilemma and ambiguity are, of course, at the very centre of learning, individual and organisational, and it is this constant grappling with complexity that makes schools interesting and dynamic places. Effective schools, in their myriad forms, never stay still long enough to be pinned down.

Nevertheless, it has been widely seen as important to try to pin schools down and for three decades we have tried to get to grips with the questions, 'What are the essential ingredients of effective schools?' and 'What makes one school more effective than another?' The two groups most absorbed with this question have been researchers and policy-makers; researchers because it is their job to find answers to their own questions; policy-makers because they want answers which will justify their decisions. While researchers treat the answers as problematic, policy-makers take them as axiomatic. And schools are at the receiving end of this two-step process to greater effectiveness.

The only problem is that it does not work like that and cannot work like that because there are laws of learning, the first of which is that learners construct knowledge for themselves. The same applies to organisations. Learners and learning organisations construct learning in their own context and by dealing with the contingencies which they face in their daily work. The external reference point provided by school effectiveness research is vital but it can be made sense of only in context and only when there is enough prior learning to render it engaging and meaningful.

The quest for the effective school has generated many lists. It has also generated lists of lists, ranging from Borger's sparse study of three[2] to Scheerens and Bosker's generous review of over seven hundred.[3] Most of these lists tend to agree on the substantive core items which teachers generally find unexceptionable, if somewhat unexciting, since they seem to do no more than confirm good sense, if not 'common' sense. Few could take issue with the list of eleven factors produced by Pam Sammons and her colleagues at the London Institute of Education.[4]

1 shared vision and goals
2 a learning environment
3 positive reinforcement
4 concentration on teaching and learning
5 monitoring progress
6 a learning organisation
7 professional leadership
8 home – school partnership
9 purposeful teaching
10 high expectations
11 pupil rights and responsibilities

In itself, the list of factors is of limited help to a school or to teachers. This may be for a variety of different reasons:

- because many of these seem too far removed from the day-to-day concerns of the classroom teacher
- because the criteria are difficult to grasp without a fuller, more discursive treatment
- because there is no immediate opportunity, context or lever for the teacher to use in applying these
- because they are not seen as interesting, valid or relevant
- because it is undermining to be presented with criteria which you have no control over
- because the underlying research methodology is not easy to gain access to or understand

Where factors of school effectiveness come from, and how they are arrived at, is likely to be a mystery for many teachers, however much they may have immediate appeal to common sense. Typically, school effectiveness characteristics are the product of studies in which researchers look at a group of schools (Rutter *et al.*'s twelve[5] or Mortimore *et al.*'s fifty[6]), identifying those features which tend to be found in the 'more effective' schools; that is, those schools whose pupils perform relatively well on standardised tests. While measures of attitudes are often used as well, the term 'effective' is generally used to refer to high standardised attainment after background factors have been taken into account. Thus, in study after study, we find that the more effective schools tend also to be associated with a cluster of common features such as high expectations, home–school partnerships, professional leadership, an orderly environment and so on.

Where researchers find 'variance' among schools which are closely matched in terms of background factors, the variance between them can largely be explained in terms of that cluster of factors which seems to emerge consistently from their statistical analyses.[7]

A natural conclusion from this evidence might be that, other things being equal, pupils are better off in an orderly environment than in a disorderly one, more inclined to do well under effective than ineffective leadership, more predisposed to achieve success when there are high expectations, and better off in a school where there is a shared vision among the staff. Yet the presence of such factors is, of itself, no guarantee of a good school experience for all pupils, nor is there a guarantee that a school lacking some of these characteristics will not provide a rewarding place for some of its pupils. Indeed, schools which offer exceptions to the rule might prove to be a most challenging area for research.

School effects researchers are always careful to add a disclaimer to their conclusions. They point out that effectiveness factors are not explanations but correlations. So, for example, one primary school study[8] found that headteachers' high expectations correlated 0.49 with high achievement. In another[9] it was found that an 'orderly and secure school climate' correlated 0.34 with student achievement. So, while there is a connection, it is a fairly tentative one and of most significance is the interrelationship of these factors. In the real world of schools, these dimensions of school culture do not have lives of their own but are interdependent and cumulative. The whole is always larger than the sum of the parts.

Whether we are talking about national cultures or organisational cultures, the caveat from Hampden-Turner and Trompenaars is important to bear in mind: 'The culture that puts parts before wholes is left with the pieces: statistics without meaning, inventories without purpose, tasks without integration, functions without co-ordination ... a rationality of parts an irrationality of the whole organisation.'[10]

Taken together in dynamic combination, Sammons et al.'s eleven factors listed above are likely to provide a fairly robust set of benchmarks for an effective school but they cannot tell the whole story. Indeed, researchers are the first to complain when policy-makers rush in with neat and tidy blueprints for improvement.

Caution must also be exercised when talking about 'the school' as if it were some kind of homogeneous entity; as if it were the same place for all its pupils. This has been an issue of particular interest to researchers over the last few years and more recent studies (including the ground-breaking longitudinal research by Pam Sammons and her colleagues at London's Institute of Education[11]) have explored 'differential effectiveness', confirming that within most schools there are eddies of excellence and stagnant backwaters. Some groups of pupils do better than others. Some show spurts of achievement, some reach a plateau and stay there, others regress. Some individual pupils thrive with individual teachers or do well in some subject departments and not others. Girls *tend* to do better overall than boys. They do significantly better in some subjects and marginally better in others. Some boys outdo girls in everything.

The Sammons et al. longitudinal study also revealed complex patterns of achievement, ebbs and flows over time. For example, as pupils moved up through the system, the influence of social class became more pronounced. Differences among ethnic groups provided a much more complex picture. Among children from a Caribbean background, for example, reading attainment lagged further and further behind in the junior school years but the trend was reversed in secondary. In secondary school, children of Chinese, Indian, Pakistani and Bangladeshi origin make better progress than their white peers. A study by the Association of Metropolitan Authorities found that schools which obtained higher than average results for the most able (in other words, 'more effective' schools) were ineffective for the least able.[12]

Ability, class, ethnicity and gender can, for the purposes of research, be isolated as independent factors but it is the interrelationship of these that is the most significant. The experience of a low-attaining English middle-class girl with parents of Indian background needs to be probed with a more textured understanding of peer-group affiliation, racial and sexual harassment, ascribed roles, subcultural tensions and parental and teacher expectations. High-achieving, African-Caribbean boys may experience particularly acute difficulties in adjusting to the different expectations of peers, teachers, their families and the group identity which defines them not only as a threat to the authority of teachers but to that of the police and others in positions of power.

A review of recent research provides a rich and detailed picture of the intersection between individual experience and school life.[13] Drawing on both school effectiveness research and ethnographic studies, the authors conclude that we have still some way to go in understanding how the internal culture of the school works and how it connects – in multiple, interwoven strands – to the world outside.

Taken together, the effectiveness and ethnographic research are highly significant and important for teachers. They both refine and expose the weaknesses in our understanding. They provide a frame of reference for teachers to examine the intricate interplay of the gender, ethnic and social class factors in their own classrooms. These insights can be put to the service of management. They can help to reassess whole-school policies and practice, for example, with regard to discipline, harassment, homework, learning difficulties and study support. To do justice to the issues, however, requires specific information at school and classroom level which can be used in conjunction with more general data. Information needs to be complemented by practical strategies which teachers can use to enhance learning and demonstrate improvement for all pupils.

A MATTER OF CONTEXT?

In the continuing quest for the unicorn, we have discovered just how much context, ecology and individual experience matter. No matter how much we search for universal laws, human beings will always find creative exceptions. Charles Hampden-Turner and Fons Trompenaars have this to say about universal laws: 'The integrity of an enterprise, its value to stakeholders, must depend on how well universalism (rules of wide generality) is reconciled with particularism (special exceptions).'[14] They also warn of the universal product:

> The headlong pursuit of the universal product, the automated factory, the ultra efficient office tends to eclipse particular persons, unique relationships, special circumstances, and exceptional request (particularism). Similarly the urge to analyse and reduce everything to basics neglects the appreciation of wholes, of harmonies, designs, aesthetics, and superordinate bonds (integration).[15]

School effects researchers have also discovered that some indicators do not travel well across international borders. Leadership of the headteacher is one example. It emerges consistently as a factor in effectiveness studies but leadership is peculiar to certain countries. In Swiss primary schools there is commonly no headteacher, only a lead teacher who takes on minor administrative duties. In Dutch schools heads have responsibility for a cluster of schools, and the large body of Dutch research on school effectiveness does not include leadership as a significant factor. Nor does the headteacher figure large in Danish schools where there is a long-standing democratic tradition, a 'flatarchy' of administration and a cultural belief in shared leadership. A recent Danish visitor to this country found it astonishing that a school with twelve teachers was falling apart because it had lost its head (an apt turn of phrase perhaps) and the new headteacher had not yet arrived. It was, for the Danish visitor, a symptom of learned helplessness.

We have learned from our study of leadership that a good head in school A may, when she moves to school B, become a good head in an entirely different way, or might not be such a good head at all.[16] Women tend to be effective in different ways from men. The apparent effectiveness of a head in one school may simply be the reflection of a very competent deputy or a secretary who manages him or her well.

A child who moves from one school to another does not move just from the bailiwick of one head to another, nor just into the province of a different set of staff, but into a different peer-group environment. This may prove to be the most telling factor of all in terms of achievement and attitudes. In fact, effectiveness studies confirm the importance of the 'compositional' or 'contextual' effect, referring to the dynamic critical mass, the point at which individual achievement falls or rises depending on who your peers are and how many of them are high or low achievers. As Douglas Willms showed in the Scottish context, when high-achieving pupils leave, some of the school's positive energy source is drained off.[17] Further, when high-achieving pupils leave to go to a 'better' school, they may also take with them their more assertive parents and further drain the school of a potential energy or irritant source.

A MATTER OF COMMUNITY

The further we venture into this complex territory, the more we discover about community, family and neighbourhood effects. The more we discover, the more we know about what pupils bring with them into the classroom and take away with them to their homes. What they bring with them is a groundbed of atti-tudes, beliefs and convictions on which the seeds of knowledge sit, take root or are quickly washed away.

'Schools Make a Difference' is incorporated into the titles of more than one book.[18] It is a title chosen to counteract the pessimism of earlier school effects studies. It is, in this sense, a 'political title. Its self-consciously upbeat message carries with it a warning for teachers, however. Some politicians and policy-makers have chosen to read this as 'schools make *all* the difference' and have consequently placed on classroom teachers an intolerable burden of responsibility.

The truth is that what happens outside schools matters more. The most effective school can make a difference of something like two GCSEs compared with the least effective school. While this can be translated into a significant difference for some individual young people, long-term, sustainable improvement for all can only be vouchsafed when there are powerful alliances with family and community.

As research into the contextual effect reveals, the internal community of the school is a milieu for the development of attitudes, expectations and sense of self; but it cannot be understood in isolation from the wider community. Ten years or more of growing up in a community of your peers and influential adults spurs on or retards motivation and achievement, but it is the nature of the movement between the communities of school and home that shapes the present and sets out the pathway to individual futures.

James Coleman, the man who first raised the question of school effects back in 1966, returned thirty years later to pursue a finding that had intrigued researchers for a decade or more – that pupils in church schools tended to do better than pupils in non-church schools.[19] He concluded that it was not, in fact, a 'school effect' but a 'church effect'. That is to say, children performed better in schools if they already had experience within a structured community of adults and children such as a church provides. That milieu, argued Coleman, helped to mediate children's experience and made it easier for them to cope with the structured, systematic environment of the school.

The Israeli researcher Reuven Feuerstein reached a similar conclusion.[20] Poverty was not, of itself, the determining factor in school achievement or failure, he concluded. The critical factor was the structure of relationships between adults and children in the home and community. Where parents or other adults mediated children's experience, children came to school better equipped to cope with structured and sequenced learning. The emphasis given to out-of-school learning by the Blair government is a recognition of the '15–85' factor. This refers to the proportion of time that children spend in school and out of it. Coincidentally, perhaps, it also refers to the relative impact of the school effect as against the non-school effect as has been consistently identified by researchers over a thirty-year period.

A MATTER OF VALUES?

The search for effective schools is not a value-free activity. The term 'effective' is not a neutral term, however much researchers try to invest it with scientific or technical meaning. While the purists argue that 'effective' has an objective meaning while 'good' is a subjective term, in point of fact both are value-judgements. Both start from a set of premises as to what school is for, how its success should be judged and by what means.

The definition of an effective school, widely accepted among researchers, is Peter Mortimore's: 'one in which pupils progress further than might be expected from consideration of its intake.'[21] This definition is useful and lends clarity and specificity to the school effect as measured in attainment terms. Its specificity may also create a problem, however, if it is used to exclude other ways of being effective. Peter Mortimore has been one of the strongest advocates for a broader view of achievement but the input/output model (measure starting point A, measure end point B and subtract the difference) lends itself less easily to vital but difficult-to-measure educational qualities. For example, 'value-added values' might be much more at the heart of what education is about but is almost certainly an unattainable measure in any reliable quantitative sense.

Some might argue, perfectly reasonably, that a truly 'effective' school would be one in which its pupils, from however tough or violent a background, developed into exemplary moral and social beings. Using the input/output model and applying Mortimore's definition, the effectiveness of the school would be gauged in terms of gains in moral achievement when set against 'prior morality' or 'social background morality'. This example of what might result when we expand the notion of effectiveness illustrates some of the difficulties researchers face in trying to objectivise school quality. The inherent weakness of the input/output model is widely recognised among school effectiveness researchers themselves but it has provided such a powerful tool for national policy-making and international comparison that matters of values and attitudes are simply excluded because they do not fit the model.

A MATTER OF PERSPECTIVE?

A 'good' school might only be good when viewed from certain angles. It may look good from the head's office but not necessarily as seen by the youngest pupil. It may not appear good from the viewpoint of the victim of bullying or the pupil struggling to cope with the demands of the curriculum. Likewise, judgements about what is 'effective' may depend on where you sit and how you define 'effective'. For the miserable and bullied child, the semantic debate on effectiveness will be of little interest. In our own Scottish study, 'Improving School Effectiveness',[22] some schools emerged as 'effective' because their mean achievement exceeded expectation and they met the criteria of the Mortimore definition. But within some of those schools, the quality of communication or professional development were, from the standpoint of teachers, seen as *in*effective. Like the 'goodness' of the schools, their effectiveness was also a matter for debate, however much our value-added data identified these as 'effective schools'.

The matter of perspective has been further illuminated by a team of Austrian researchers who developed a novel approach to self-evaluation.[23] Pupils were given a camera and asked to photograph significant hotspots in the school. They found many places in the school that took on a new meaning when seen, or captured on camera, from a pupil's-eye viewpoint. The study commented:

> Taking pictures builds a bridge to the pupils' everyday lives, especially to the feelings of young people, because usually they perceive that there is a deep abyss between their own priorities and the adults' ones. Therefore they experience an intense discrepancy between the appreciation of parts of life through themselves and through official attitudes.[24]

In a pilot study for the Scottish Office in 1991,[25] researchers were surprised by the importance placed by pupils on toilets. The weight of evidence from pupils was enough to convince the Inspectorate that this was not a matter of peripheral concern but a significant index of school culture. Yet it is an item conspicuously absent in school effectiveness lists and there is no substantive literature on the subject. Is this because it has not been factored into the research or because a correlation between quality of toilets and measured attainment would be hard to establish? Its absence suggests a top-down perspective on schools because toilets do not figure large in how adults view schools. Their focus is more narrowly on the formal and 'intended' aspects of schools rather than on school life as experienced by pupils or, for that matter, by teachers.

The issue of vantage point on effectiveness came into sharp focus at a conference in Pisa in April 1998 which brought together headteachers, teacher organisations, parents and school students for three days to discuss quality in education. A report from that conference describes the tension between the top-down and bottom-up viewpoints:

> The central theme and tenor of the debate was set on day one. In an open-ing panel discussion, the fuse was lit by a Finnish headteacher who made her own bold claim for 'knowing best'. After twenty-two years of much water and many bridges, she could say with complete conviction that she knew her school. This brought a swift rejoinder from a 16-year-old Dutch delegate. Mounting the platform and politely borrowing the mike he said, 'I have sat in classrooms six periods a day for thirty weeks a year for five years and, with respect, I see things you could never see. These five years and thousands of hours are my life in school. They are my one chance.[26]

The beauty of it is that both are right. Who could argue with the head? Who could deny the validity of the student's experience? If we are serious about evaluating quality and standards in schools, this dialogue is at the very heart of the issue. The danger lies in the either/or. It lies in the definitive and dogmatic judgements, whether from headteachers, students or school inspectors. Each of these brings a perspective, a lens, a vantage point from which to view the school. The head-teacher takes a bird's-eye view while the student sees it from the worm's eye. The inspector brings an outsider's viewpoint, a third eye. It is the juxtaposition of these viewpoints which brings new insights, new ways of seeing. The willingness to treat all of those perspectives with concern for evidence and openness to challenge is, in itself, a model of educational process. A culture of school improvement is one which nourishes the quality of that dialogue.

A MATTER OF PURPOSE

What purpose, political or otherwise, is the driving motive for evaluation? What impelled the three-decade-long quest for effective schools? Was it for purely dis-interested academic motives, a search after truth? Was it to contest previous research findings? Was it to inform policy; in other words, driven by 'political' motives? Was it to endorse the policies of political parties?

If schools, authorities or national bodies are to use the findings of school effectiveness research as a reference point, we need to be aware of the covert or overt purpose. Some of these might be:

- for accountability purposes
- for comparative purposes (locally, nationally or internationally)
- for marketing purposes
- for diagnostic and formative purposes

As we become more aware of the diverse purposes of evaluation, we become more aware of the misuse or abuse of the findings. One misuse is for inspectors to take it as a template or checklist for monitoring schools and on this basis for holding teachers accountable. It is also a questionable practice for a school to use such a list for its own internal evaluation because, like any list, any set of criteria, it needs to be worked at, examined critically, tested and, above all, invested with meaning from people's own individual experiences.

This is the predominant theme from school improvement research which has sought to go beyond a pure effectiveness approach, both to ascertain how schools improve and to assist them in the process. One commentator presents two cartoon caricatures illustrating differences between effectiveness researchers and those working in the field of school improvement.[27] One depicts a person seated at a computer, the other shows someone sitting in the staff room chatting with a teacher over a cup of coffee. The kernel of truth in the caricature is that improvers are less interested in the characteristics of effectiveness than in the dynamics of change, with reflective dialogue among teachers playing a significant role. The flaw in the caricature is that most people working in effectiveness and improvement fields now see these as complementary strands and believe that we must move beyond the simplistic dichotomy between outcomes and process, quantitative and qualitative data, 'pure' and 'applied' research. The key test for school improvement, suggests Michael Huberman, is whether the investment in staff development and enhancing of school culture works itself down to the 'end of the chain' with benefits for the learning of every single child.

A MATTER OF COMPARISON

The use of school effectiveness methodology to compare the performance of nations is a preoccupation of politicians but it is based on assumptions unsupported by evidence and dependent on questionable indices. Policy-makers find international comparisons compelling because the data are likely to be used as a stick with which to beat government performance, whether by the opposition or by the press. The OECD has created an international industry and ministers from every nation keenly await publication, demanding action and answers from civil servants when we compare unfavourably with Singapore, Korea or Japan.[28] Yet the two major problems of such international comparisons are largely ignored.

The first problem is the lack of evidence to connect test performance at school level with economic performance at national level. Were test and economic performances to correlate, countries with a poor economy would not perform well in standardised tests while in rich countries the opposite would be the case. Comparing the Gross National Product (GNP) of countries with mean attainment scores in mathematics, Peter Robinson (chief economist at the Institute for Public Policy Research) demonstrates the total lack of correlation. South Korea, for example, second in attainment, is close to the bottom in GNP. Kuwait, second highest in GNP, is near the very bottom in terms of pupils' achievement. Describing 'the hunt for scapegoats', Robinson concludes: 'In the past the scapegoats have included the City of London and the anti-industrial bias of the English culture. The current favourite scapegoat is the education system.'[29]

The historical roots of this go back as far as the launch of the Russian Sputnik in 1957 which sparked off in the United States a series of curriculum initiatives, reviews and federal programmes to raise standards. Alarm bells were sounded again in 1983 with the US National Commission's publication of 'Nation at Risk' in which schools were blamed for the country's declining performance in the world economy.[30] Yet, as many commentators have since pointed out, when the US economy began to boom in the 1990s it was not ascribed to schools' performance; nor was the relative decline in the Pacific Rim economies explained in this way. As the economist Clark Kerr comments: 'seldom in the course of policy making in the United States have so many firm convictions held by so many been based on so little proof.'[31]

Yet we, among many other countries, have complied with this problematic course and seem happy, or resigned, to follow where America has led.

The second major problem is how inferences are drawn from comparative data. If, for example, British schools perform less well than Japanese schools, does this mean that schools themselves are actually 'worse', or might explanations of differential performance lie elsewhere? Describing the Japanese culture, Gerald Bracey writes: 'Children in Japan often come home from public schools at 3.30 in the afternoon, eat and go on to private school or tutor. They attend school on Saturdays and many go on Sundays as well.'[32]

In fact, there are 35,000 such private tutorial schools in Japan. Describing educational practice in another Pacific Rim tiger, Singapore, Bracey goes on to describe how guest workers there leave their children behind to be educated in their own countries. And while parents whose children are not doing well in Singapore's schools are sometimes sent to Malaysia, Malaysian children who do well on tests are admitted to Singapore schools. Describing Singapore's education Bracey concludes: 'Singapore may well get its high scores by exporting low achieving students while importing high achieving students.'[33]

Irrespective of whether Bracey's analysis holds up, Singapore's ministers themselves are increasingly aware of the view that pushing students to study for the sake of good grades has been a failing and that student burnout is the high price which the country is paying for its leading place in the international ranking. Opening the World Conference on Thinking Skills in 1997, Prime Minister Goh Chok Tong said,

> What is critical is that we fire in our students a passion for learning, instead of studying for the sake of getting good grades in their examinations. Their knowledge will be fragile, no matter how many As they get . . . It is the capacity to learn that will define excellence in the future not simply what young people achieve in school.[34]

A MATTER OF THINKING

There are many, and ever multiplying, school effectiveness and improvement projects. Each seems to generate its own conceptual framework, usually with something between eight and twelve indicators, themes or categories. The simple answer for a school would be to take one of the many frameworks, Sammons *et al.*'s eleven listed above or the National Commission's twelve,[35] rather than 'reinventing the wheel'. The problem with such an approach is that conceptual frameworks do not make sense simply on paper or in the abstract. They have to be made sense of inside people's heads and through dialogue between people. No matter how elegant a framework might be, it will almost always be modified and de- or re-constructed. And so it should be. Like any piece of knowledge, it is made meaningful by being remade.

Any conceptual model, any framework or attempt at development or improvement, must respect those fundamental tenets. It must

- start from teachers' own experiences and understanding
- have some purpose which makes sense
- respect and relate to the context of teachers' work
- have a structure which helps to make sense of experience

Motivational theory also provides us with evidence on why people (pupils, teachers, and anyone else, for that matter) lose, or fail to acquire, motivation. Charles Desforges offers the following four reasons:

- the person does not possess the knowledge they are thought to have
- knowledge has been acquired but its relevance to a new problem is not seen
- the relevance of available knowledge is seen but the application strategy is not available
- the strategy is available but the learner lacks the self-confidence or will to make the effort to succeed[36]

The starting point with teachers, therefore, is, how they see their schools, what is important to them, their criteria of effectiveness or, quite simply, the question what makes a school 'good'? Teachers' views will, in some cases, be half-formed, inadequate or contradictory, but that is the baseline for their learning. Only the most arrogant can claim that they know it all. It is truly dangerous when people in positions of power, whether at national, school or classroom level, fit the following definition: 'a mind so well equipped with the means of refutation that no new idea has the tenacity to seek admittance.'[37]

Teachers, like inspectors, policy-makers and politicians, work from implicit theories; that is, taken-for-granted beliefs and intuitions that underpin their professional lives and shape their daily practice. In a 'professional' context, we would see that axiomatic theories need to be explicit rather than implicit. If they are in the open, they can be examined, and tested and reshaped if need be. This is one of the primary purposes of self-evaluation.

A MATTER OF HOW

Sammons *et al.*'s eleven-point list is an important and useful digest of school effectiveness research but it does not go beyond the 'what' nor has pretensions to do so. The pertinent question for schools is the 'how' question. Once we have identified high expectations as important, how do we acquire them? What are the chemistry and physics of expectations? The NUT research gave us some of the answers to that question from the perspective of pupils. They knew which teachers did and did not help them set high standards or pushed them to exceed their own expectations. Pupils were perceptive about what those teachers did in practice and razor sharp in their critique of teachers who lowered their sights and patronised them.

Pupils have an intuitive grasp of quality and have the makings of excellent ethnographers but they are not neuroscientists, organisational psychologists or teachers with twenty years' experience of classrooms. To answer the 'how' question, we have to go to those sources as well, to find out what works, to test practice against theory and theory against practice.

There is a large and ever-larger literature on accelerated learning, super learning, suggestopaedics, neuro-linguistic programming and organisational learning.[38] The best of it is practical, grounded in research and infused by good theory. For schools which want to become effective, this literature provides an important and necessary complement to the insights of the internal stakeholders and school effectiveness researchers. If we wish to meet Sammons *et al.*'s criteria one and six, these are indispensable sources.

3

HOW THE FRAMEWORK WAS DEVELOPED

The 1995 study

The commission by the National Union of Teachers in 1995 was to work together with a group of schools to develop a school-friendly but robust approach to self-evaluation. Drawing on earlier work in Scottish schools, the research team was asked to consider what part teachers, pupils, parents and other groups could play in the production of their own frameworks and instruments for self-evaluation.

We wanted to learn from the experience of individual schools, to test out ideas with them and to tease out from those experiences common strands and collective insights on the characteristics of 'good' schools. We saw it as important that any framework for self-evaluation should take careful account of the people who *are* the schools and carry the responsibility for their success and improvement. In other words, as well as being subject to reports published by OFSTED or other external agencies, those responsible for the management of schools should be enabled to render *their* accounts of their school's performance. Similarly, teachers and pupils should be enabled to render their account of what makes for effective learning, while the expectations and perspectives of parents and governors should be an integral ingredient in the mix.

We also recognised the tension between a need for self-evaluation and the energy required to put it into effect: the tension between genuine ownership of the criteria by which schools are to be judged and the inherent dangers of squandering that most precious resource – time – in 'reinvention of the wheel'.

Our task, therefore, was to:

- help schools to identify criteria which were realistic, meaningful and which referred to essential purposes of school education
- help schools to create a climate in which the process would be seen as energising rather than enervating, and motivating for all parties involved
- provide starting points and guidelines without being unnecessarily directive
- develop a framework robust enough to be credible in a range of contexts but flexible enough to meet the needs of individual schools

In the schools we worked with, we started from a blank sheet, without preconceptions about what various groups would say. We wanted the evidence to speak for itself. Having gathered and analysed the evidence, we then examined the findings in the context of wider research into school effectiveness and improvement.

DEVELOPING A FRAMEWORK

It was agreed that the research team would work in a sample of ten schools in England and Wales during the months of June and July 1995. The schools were selected to cover as representative a range as possible. There were six primary schools geographically spread from London to Newcastle and secondary schools in London, Canterbury and Wales. There was also a special school in Leeds. The schools covered the socio-economic spectrum, rural and urban locations and types of school and ranged from low- to high-achieving schools. Three were multi-racial schools. One was an all-girls school. One was grant maintained.

Table 3.1 Participants in the 1995 study

	Primary/special	*Secondary*
Teachers	48	61
Management	10	16
Support staff	19	15
Pupils	201	181
Parents	67	31
Governors	24	29

GATHERING THE DATA

The initial phase of the project consisted of a systematic exploration of views on effective or 'good' schools with six key sets of players – teachers, management staff, support staff, pupils, parents and governors.

In the interests of reliability, the project team devised a framework for data gathering which could be applied in the full range of school contexts and with the various groups of respondents. We saw it as important to put the same questions to all groups and to use a format which was accessible and appropriate. There were two key questions:

- What, in your view, are the key characteristics of a 'good' school?
- Given a set of twenty-three criteria, derived from OFSTED, which of these do you rate as most important and least important for your school?

The first question was pursued by means of an open-ended task. We asked all participants to write down their own personal list of five 'die-in-the-ditch indicators' of a good school. With pupils or parents who had language or writing difficulties, brainstorming of items was used instead. Very young children were asked to draw or paint what they liked and disliked about the school. Primary pupils were also asked to produce a short list of what they thought made a good teacher.

In secondary schools there was a follow-up activity. People were asked to work in groups of five to six with a set of cards, each card holding a criterion taken from the OFSTED 'New Framework for School Inspection'. The groups were asked to spread the cards out on the table and to agree on the five they regarded as most important, and the three which they saw as least important.

These various activities left us with a substantial body of data. The total number of indicators suggested for the good school came to 1,743. We had many lists of what made a good teacher and large numbers of drawings and paintings from younger children on good and less good things about their schools. There were, in addition, 392 priorities which emerged from the OFSTED card sorts.

All the activities were followed up by a discussion of what lay behind people's choices, with us – as critical friends – probing, questioning and enjoying the animated discussion which always seemed to emerge from the exercise. In every case, these discussions could easily have exceeded the allotted time span but they had to be curtailed to allow for the final phase of the exercise. This was concerned with how each school might gather evidence to evaluate the extent to which its own suggested criteria were being met.

ISSUES OF CONTENT AND PROCESS

Although we were gathering a material body of data, we were also trying out and modelling a process for gathering data. The twin focuses – What are the criteria for judging a good school? and How do you rank the OFSTED criteria? – were found by participants and the research team to be appropriate and practical. They proved to be both productive and flexible as mechanisms for eliciting the views of the various groups in the wide range of different contexts.

The process yielded important and illuminating insights. It confirmed experience from elsewhere that 'stakeholders' in schools welcome discussion and clarification of priorities as challenging, empowering and important in the context of their own school's development.

There are clearly limitations to the validity of data generated in this way. The data cannot provide a generalisable account of the views of all parents, teachers or pupils in English and Welsh schools. Nor can the views emerging from the prioritisation of the OFSTED criteria be taken as representative or definitive. It proved, nonetheless, to be an immensely powerful and useful way of generating dialogue and raising issues. It was experienced by adults and young people as empowering and words like 'uplifting', 'challenging', 'fun' and 'exciting' were frequently used to describe the process.

We found it to be an engaging and friendly way of exploring important themes but also one with a real cutting edge. It is a process which schools themselves can undertake and we are confident that it is both practical and manageable. The self-evaluation process does not require specific research skills but does rely on the repertoire of abilities that a good teacher, interviewer or counsellor can bring. That is, it requires an ability to listen, to prompt, to question and to create a climate of openness and trust. In all schools the process itself was regarded as valuable by participants. Almost without exception, they said they were pleased to have been involved and grateful for the recognition and respect given to their views.

GENERATING THE INDICATORS

The task presented – provide your own indicators of a good school – generated 1,743 different criteria and more than 300 individual lists. Each of these lists was unique in that no two people had the same five items worded in exactly the same way. Each list also had its own internal logic and its own value system. This can be illustrated by the following six examples from a teacher, a pupil, a parent, a member of support staff, a governor and a member of the senior management team. It shows issues held in common and issues specific to a particular standpoint. These are chosen as fairly typical examples of what people wrote when asked to give their own five indicators of a good school.

Pupils

- pupils are nice to each other
- everyone is treated fairly
- there is a friendly atmosphere
- teachers who can control the class but are not too strict
- teachers who help you with things you are not good at

Teachers

- good communication among all members
- good staff development and school INSET
- a good environment to work in (buildings, repairs, presentation)
- pupils are happy and well motivated
- helps all pupils to achieve what they're capable of

Parents

- there is a welcoming friendly atmosphere
- a caring staff who communicate well with pupils
- good discipline
- extra time is spent with children who learn less quickly
- good relationships between teachers and parents

Management

- pupils feel safe
- all members of the school community work towards clear objectives
- a high quality of information to parents and visitors
- rules are applied evenly and fairly
- helps all pupils to achieve what they're capable of

Support staff

- good up-to-date resources
- classrooms are clean, warm and comfortable
- support staff are given credit for their competence and contribution
- the environment is friendly and welcoming
- staff development involves all staff

Governors

- excellent reputation with the local community
- strong leadership from senior management
- a happy and welcoming environment
- pupils being helped to reach their individual potential
- a safe place for pupils and teachers

These individual examples shed some light on particular viewpoints and the balance of emphasis within each of those. Looking across the different sets, the examples also help to identify concerns which are held in common or are unique to different groups. They are a starting point for a closer examination of specific perspectives from different groups. That is, are there common issues among teachers as a group, among pupils, among parents, or among governors?

The analysis of indicators group by group reveals some indicators that are unique to a specific group and others where it is more a matter of emphasis or priority. Home–school links were never mentioned by pupils. Common rooms and toilets were never mentioned by teachers. All groups were concerned with safety but it was a much greater concern among pupils and parents. All gave some mention to the importance of good working relationships among staff, but it was more of an issue for teachers and support staff than for parents or pupils.

Our task was to take these disparate sets of indicators and put them together into some kind of systematic order, identifying the common themes but taking care not to lose the specific and individual concerns.

Differences of viewpoint are frequently at the root of misunderstandings and conflicts. They tend to be dealt with in terms of their surface manifestations rather than with a deeper understanding of why they are necessarily different. The differences of priority from one group to the next provide us with an interesting form of challenge for developing a framework because they start with the concerns and priorities of people rather than with the structures of 'the system'.

The differences in priority remind us that although the school is a school, it is, in some crucial respects, a quite different place for different people. For teachers, the school is their place of work. They have expectations about their working environment and about the attitudes of others towards them as 'teachers'. They have their own places where only teachers go and where they mix exclusively with their colleagues. Work bases and staff rooms play an important part in the teacher culture within the school and provide a context in which attitudes to pupils, parents and education are tested and shaped.

Pupils use the school's buildings and resources in different ways from their teachers. They have few, if any, places that are theirs and many places they cannot go without permission. They live much of the day in a different culture – the pupil culture – often hidden from teachers, even within the classroom. If management and teachers can be said to have a bird's-eye view of the school then pupils have a worm's eye view, and the younger they are, the closer to the ground that view is. They see the school from the bottom up. Parents have a different perspective again. They are only occasional visitors to the building in a physical sense but they have a vicarious existence in the school, lived through the experience of their children.

If we then start the process of building an indicator set with one group and one set of perspectives, we can overlay this with other group perspectives as we go along, eventually arriving at one common set, but a common set which accommodates differences.

Using our data from pupils as the basis for our set of indicators yields a scheme as represented in Diagram 3.1.

In this scheme of things there are seven interlocking spheres, each of which contains a cluster of different individual items. Time and resources, for example, bring together all references to materials, equipment, things to use, places to go and time to use these resources. The two most important spheres are *support for learning* and *school climate* because they represent clusters of items emphasised most frequently by pupils, either in their indicator list or in follow-up discussion. These two central spheres are linked together by *classroom climate*, a cluster of items which includes indicators such as 'A classroom where you can get on with your work peacefully' and 'Do teachers make the classroom a nice place to be in?'

The four clusters at the corners – *recognition of achievement, equity, relationships, time and resources* – are all related to these three central features and, in the real world, are inextricable from them. We have put them into separate categories because they were frequently given specific mention by pupils. A fuller description

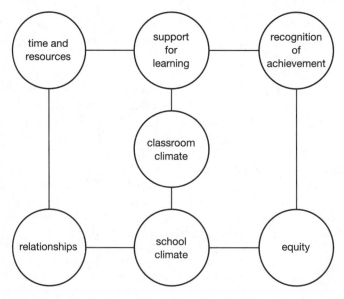

Diagram 3.1 Pupils' indicator set

of what is contained in each of these clusters is provided in the list from page 33 onwards, and Chapter 4 deals in more detail with some of the deeper meanings and significance which underlie these sometimes terse descriptors.

Diagram 3.2 shows the schema from a teacher's point of view. Like pupils, teachers mentioned school climate more often than any other single indicator. Closely related were values and procedures which made teaching not only possible but congenial, for example, 'the school values teaching' and 'teaching strategies are discussed and shared among staff'. These were related to *organisation and communication, relationships, time and resources*, and *recognition of achievement* (for staff as well as pupils) but we have made them into separate categories to emphasise their importance and allow them to be specific foci of evaluation.

The same procedure may also be followed for parents, support staff, senior management or governors. In each case the schema looks slightly different. For parents, home and school issues loomed larger. Support staff emphasised resources, relationships and organisational issues. Governors shared that concern for organisational issues and school leadership but also stressed relations with the external community. Senior staff made more of whole-school climate, whole-school planning and staff development.

When we map these different clusters on to one another we arrive at a common schema as depicted in Diagram 3.3. It cannot begin to encapsulate the richness and diversity of what people wrote and said, but it is an attempt to limit and condense that large repertory into something manageable for school self-evaluation. A tempting alternative was to borrow one of the myriad tables of classification that already exist and fit these school-based ones into that framework. In many respects they would have fitted very well because much of what was given to us closely parallels what school effectiveness researchers have been discovering for two decades. There is something to be gained, however, by trying to follow the logic of an

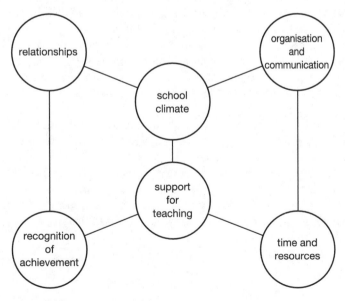

Diagram 3.2 Teachers' indicator set

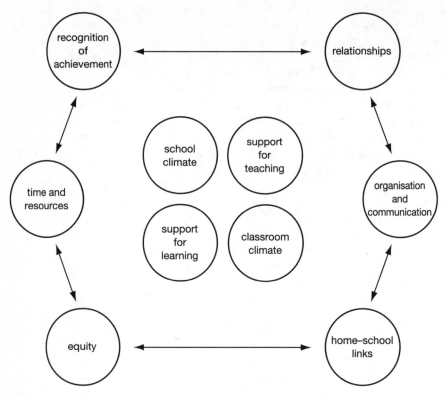

Diagram 3.3 Overall indicator set

approach that is more people-centred than system-centred and which, by retaining the original language as much as possible, brings a freshness of insight into a terminology that has become too familiar and too unproblematic.

We have chosen to depict the ten clusters in this form rather than just a list because we wanted to suggest the complex and dynamic interrelationship among the various clusters. There is no deep significance beyond that and any individual school will want to develop a schema which makes sense to them in their own context.

Within each of these ten clusters there are potentially dozens, if not hundreds, of individual indicators. For the sake of simplicity we have reduced the total indicator set to 50, 5 indicators for each of the 10 clusters. These are reproduced from pages 132 to 151. We have tried to remain faithful to the key issues as given to us, but in the final analysis it is a selective and in some respects arbitrary list. However, since we are not offering a definitive or prescriptive list but rather some key examples, whether it is completely comprehensive is not an issue. If the indicator set is used as a menu, it should be more in the nature of *à la carte* than *table d'hôte*.

THE FRAMEWORK AND PREVIOUS RESEARCH

We hope that this schema offers a useful starting point for any school embarking on self-evaluation. Using the schema as a starting point means first opening it up for debate to ascertain whether the criteria are suitable for a specific school at a specific time. This may then entail some restructuring and rewording to meet the school's own needs.

There is an inherent danger in generating school evaluation criteria from people's opinions and spontaneous comments. Criteria generated in this way may be idiosyncratic, dissonant with what researchers have discovered about effective schools or out of step with the mainstream of policy and practice. There is a danger that such indicators will be conservative, reflecting what people have experienced rather than what might be, particularly when based on consultation with five-year-olds whose experience of the alternatives is necessarily somewhat limited!

Perhaps developing yet another framework for school evaluation is, after all, both an unsound and a superfluous exercise. There are many good ones that exist and that are grounded in long-term rigorous and systematic research. There are researchers who have given time to a secondary analysis of all major research studies conducted, and who have produced syntheses of the most consistent robust findings. Despite all of this, the evidence is that, as in any approach to learning, personal insight and understanding are at the roots of commitment. In all of the ten schools we worked with there was an engagement with the exercise from the level of the five-year-old to the retiring chair of the governing body. It was an interest that would have been hard to generate with a predetermined set of criteria. This does not mean that each school has to start from scratch, but it does mean there has to be some way of adopting or adapting the criteria. A sifting and prioritisation of existing OFSTED criteria accompanied by vigorous debate is one shorter cut to that destination.

When a school, or a group of people within it, explores its own criteria of effectiveness it provides a much more engaging basis for examining and understanding the research. It can confirm the value of what the school has discovered and at the same time confirm the value of the research. It may also test the research and its apparent relevance for that school. By the same token it can test the value of what the school has identified, raising questions about potential weaknesses and omissions.

Evidence can be found in the school effectiveness literature to support all of the clusters of indicators thrown up in this study. Often the research evidence is very strong. The ten indicator clusters are listed below with the research study that is most relevant to each criterion.[1]

School climate

- A safe place – Lightfoot, 1983
- Good repair and maintenance – Rutter *et al.*, 1979
- Participation in extra-curricular activities – Coleman, 1982

Relationships

- A sense of community – Purkey and Smith, 1983
- Student–teacher rapport – Trisman, 1976
- Positive teacher–pupil relations – Rutter *et al.*, 1979
- Co-operative pupil learning – Slavin, 1995

Classroom climate

- Orderly classrooms – Lipitz, 1984
- Freedom from disruption – Hersch, 1981
- Stimulating classroom environment – Walberg, 1993
- Efficient organisation of classwork – Mortimore *et al.*, 1988

Support for Teaching

- A professional culture – Hill, 1995
- Strong staff development – Purkey and Smith, 1983
- Teacher social interaction and dialogue – Little, 1988
- Small classes in early years – Achilles *et al.*, 1993
- Teachers' internal locus of control – Evertson, 1980
- Student–teacher ratio – Postlethwaite and Ross, 1992

Support for learning

- The important of praise – Brophy and Good, 1986
- Homework given out and marked – Rutter *et al.*, 1979
- Prompt feedback on homework – Turner, 1985
- Active role for teachers in helping pupils – Mortimore *et al.*, 1988
- Structure and scaffolding of learning – Slavin, 1995

Recognition of Achievement

- Achievement orientation – Brookover *et al.*, 1979
- Success is celebrated – Lipitz, 1982
- Positive reporting of achievement – Murphy 1993
- Sustained focus on success – Slavin 1995

Time and Resources

- Per pupil expenditure – Hedges, 1994
- Time is protected – Murphy, 1993
- Time for homework – Scheerens and Creemers, 1996

Organisation and communication

- Effective communication – Lee, Bryk and Smith, 1993
- Involvement of teachers in planning – Mortimore *et al.*, 1988
- Involvement of teachers in development planning – MacGilchrist *et al.*, 1995
- Effective school management team – Sammons, 1994

Equity

- Feeling of belonging – Behling, 1982
- School catering for all its pupils – Cuttance, 1987
- Targeted praise and encouragement – Smith and Tomlinson, 1989
- Opportunity to learn – Grisay, 1996

Home–School links

- Parental involvement in reading projects – Epstein, 1992
- The alterable curriculum of the home – Walberg, 1993
- Initiating contact with parents and sending home good news – Squires, 1983

There are three areas in which there is a less clear correspondence between this study and the school effectiveness evidence. These are *resources and time*, *leadership* and *equity*.

1 RESOURCES AND TIME

In the period between the original research and the follow-up study, time has become an increasingly predominant theme. Headteachers frequently described arriving at school at six in the morning and often working late into the evenings. A teacher described preparation and planning on Saturdays and Sundays. Many students found that they had to put in much of their own time often at weekends, particularly on Sundays.

School effectiveness research has consistently failed to find much association between resources and pupil achievement. This is in many cases because researchers have catalogued the existence of resources, sometimes counting books in the library and numbers of computers. Most teachers would probably agree that the mere provision of resources says little about the quality of schools. However, the way in which resources are used and the match of resources to the individual needs of the learner are fundamental to effective teaching. To have the right resources to hand can be liberating for both teacher and pupil. It would be incomprehensible in an age of technology if the availability and effective use of resources were not related to how, and how well, young people learn.

Similarly, there is a critical level at which the *use* of time is related to the *existence* of time. Time was a commodity which teachers were finding in increasingly short supply in 1995 compared with 1985 or even 1990 but it is a critical resource in the learning/teaching relationship. Time is also related to class size, with its increasing demands for assessment, differentiation, record-keeping and reporting, all of which multiply teacher time per individual pupil. The availability of time to meet the proliferating range of demands on the teacher is also clearly related to teacher morale, job satisfaction and the capacity to put children's interests first.

2 LEADERSHIP

There is a second area in which this study seems not to be clearly aligned with school effectiveness research. Whereas leadership and management are virtually constant factors in those studies, it does not appear as one of the ten categories in this study. Effective leadership or good management were rarely mentioned as such; nonetheless, their effects are implicit in many of the indicators suggested. For teachers, support from management was critical. Good organisation and communication came through a climate of trust, collaboration and shared leadership. The good school climate was important in underpinning a congenial classroom ethos, and support for learning ran continuously from the bottom to the top of the organisation. As one teacher said when we commented on the lack of explicit reference to leadership and management, 'by their fruits shall ye know them'.

3 EQUITY

School effectiveness research places strong emphasis on success for all and there is evidence to suggest that schools that are good for the minorities are schools that are good for all; for example, the 1988 Junior School Project carried out by Peter Mortimore and his team.[2] Grisay in France has also identified equity as a key factor in effective schools.[3] In the British context, however, there is very little evidence to confirm a direct relationship between equal opportunity policy, anti-racist or other anti-discrimination initiatives and measures of raised achievement. Perhaps this is because policies are of themselves no guarantee of equal treatment or perhaps because to be free of sexual and racial harassment is an end in itself and may provide the seedbed for raised achievement in the longer term.

Irrespective of whether clear associations are found between a commitment to equality and measured attainment, we can assert from our evidence that a prior concern of parents is that children are able to go to school in a caring environment, free from fear, and one in which they will be treated as individuals and allowed to develop their own niche. In prioritising the OFSTED criteria all groups placed a high premium on pupil needs and all groups had the individual needs of pupils somewhere near the top of their lists. Needs were interpreted by virtually everyone in a much wider sense than the need to do well on tests and exams. In their book *Making Schools More Effective*, Barry McGaw and his colleagues say:

> Above all, they [parents] want schools in which students learn to think
> well of themselves, to develop a sense of personal value and a confidence

in themselves to take them into adult life. They want competition but they want it to be with a student's own past performance not with the performance of other students.[4]

A 1989 study of parents' views in Scotland echoes these sentiments with the words of one parent:

> What I want for my children is to be what they can be, to feel at the end of their schooling, 'Well, I've got all I can out of school and now I can choose where I can go from here.' I want them to feel confident enough to be able to choose because they have to make the decisions, and the decisions they make on leaving school will have ripples throughout the rest of their life.[5]

A school developing its own criteria for self-evaluation is, of course, engaged in a different kind of exercise from researchers, and the purposes of the self-evaluation must be kept in mind. It is about needs, not only of pupils but of teachers and parents. It is about a range of things which supersede pupil achievement but are also preconditions for that. Keeping the needs of young people, their families and their teachers at the forefront was the message that came across to us in all the ten very different schools.

THE TEN INDICATORS AT A GLANCE

1 School climate

At the centre lies school climate because that was mentioned most often by all groups. The words 'atmosphere', 'climate' or 'ethos' were often used specifically, more so by teachers and parents, less so by secondary students and hardly at all by primary pupils. There were, however, many references by them to the school as a friendly place and allusions to how a school 'is' or 'feels'. We have included all of these within the category of 'school climate'.

2 Relationships

We have put relationships into a separate category because they were mentioned frequently and specifically as determining characteristics of a good school. The most common form of relationship mentioned was that of student–teacher but staff were just as likely to mention collegial relationships, relationships between teaching and support staff or between teaching staff and senior management.

3 Organisation and communication

School climate and relationships are obviously affected by organisation and communication in the school. We have made this a category on its own because of references made (more so by staff than any other group) to the efficiency of communication among staff and between staff and senior management.

4 Time and resources

The efficiency of organisation and communication bear some relationship to resources and to time as a critical resource to be deployed well or badly. Mentions were made (more often by students than other groups) of 'materials', 'equipment' and 'opportunities and time to use them'.

5 Recognition of achievement

Student achievement is, for most people, a chief purpose of the school, but it meant recognising and rewarding effort and excellence in a range of different ways. Criteria suggested by all groups emphasised the value of this as all-inclusive rather than for the select few. Under this heading, we have included recognition of staff achievement too because it was mentioned a number of times in conjunction with student achievement as a hallmark of the genuinely positive and rewarding climate.

6 Equity

We have used the term 'equity' to cover a range of meanings. It referred to the school's openness to disabled people and the opportunity to succeed for those who had special needs. It referred to being treated equally regardless of gender, race or academic ability. For students, it was often expressed as being treated fairly and not being picked on by teachers.

7 Home–school links

Equity and achievement were issues that, perhaps more than any others, crossed the home–school divide because schools have to be careful not to compound the failure of children already disadvantaged by home and community background. We have used this category to describe all references to parental involvement, exchange of information between home and school or mentions of support and partnership.

8 Support for teaching

For teachers, home–school links were important for supporting teaching but reference was also made to a much wider set of conditions which supported the teacher. Some had to do with time and resources, some to do with relationships, some referred to staff development time. We have included items in this category where mention of conditions or school infrastructure referred to helping the teacher function more effectively in the classroom. We have included class size in this category.

9 Classroom climate

There were few direct references to 'classroom climate' as such but students in particular described ways in which classrooms were stimulating or interesting places. This category includes ways in which teachers set the conditions for 'making lessons fun' or varied.

10 Support for learning

Ultimately everything in the school should work together to support young people in their learning. We have this as a category on its own because students, much more than any other group, made very specific reference to things which helped them learn – and things which hindered.

4

EXPLORING THE THEMES

In this chapter we examine the ten themes in more detail. Our discussion of these themes with different groups in the schools gave people the opportunity to elaborate on what lay behind their choice of words. These discussions led us to identify the ten themes and to derive five indicators for each of these. In other words, there is a total of fifty specific indicators. Although we might describe these fifty as the building blocks and mortar of the school, that is a limited analogy because these features of a school are as much the products as the ingredients. They arise out of beliefs, values and commitment and from the ability of school staff and governors to translate that commitment into everyday practice.

SCHOOL CLIMATE

We settled on the term 'cluster' to describe the ten themes because each comprised a cluster of five indicators. The first of these is 'school climate'. It emerged most consistently from all groups. There were 141 explicit references to 'climate', 'atmosphere', 'environment' and 'ethos'; there were a further 65 references to school as a place which was 'happy', 'caring' or 'safe'. Parents' judgements typically referred to the impressions they had when they walked in the door or visited classrooms – the warmth, the welcome, the feelings they were left with after the visit. They frequently wrote in the following kinds of terms: 'a school that is bright and welcoming'; 'the school has a buzz in its atmosphere when you go in'; 'pupils and staff greet and smile at each other when they walk down the corridor'.

For teachers, the overriding factor was the day-to-day working environment of the school and the way in which that supported or inhibited teaching and learning. They wrote about 'a caring environment', 'an atmosphere of purposeful work' and 'happy pupils and staff'.

Pupils were less likely to use the terms 'ethos' or 'climate' but they described the school as a pleasant or unpleasant place to be, and focused on those aspects which made it a more or less congenial place for learning and socialising; for example, 'where teachers treat you with respect and don't bark at you'.

Discipline and pastoral care

Discipline and pastoral care might well merit categories of their own. We have included them under 'school climate' because, in discussion with different groups, these two facets of behavioural control were often described as two sides of the same coin. They were also seen as inextricably linked to the morale and feelings of pupils and staff.

Seventy-one indicators of 'good discipline' were suggested and a further forty-four were suggested in the area of counselling, support and 'someone to go to with problems', or 'people who will listen to you before they judge you'.

A good reason for including discipline within this category was its relationship to the school as a 'safe' place, a criterion to which great importance was attached. Safety within the school was discussed in relation to harassment, bullying and intimidation from other pupils. There were twenty-three suggested indicators on bullying, twenty of them from pupils, the other three from parents. Teachers tended to set the safety issue in a wider context. In respect of the school climate they made the distinction between 'freedom from' and 'freedom to'. While freedom from fear was seen as a bottom line in any school, the freedom to take risks, take responsibility, speak out and be yourself were broader definitions of the term. A secondary school student put that wider meaning of safety into these words: 'trust in the people around you, trust and confidence in your teachers – that they will respect you as an individual, respect your opinion, respect your privacy.'

A safe and purposeful school climate was a manifestation of a well-managed school in which there was a clear structure, clear procedures and people with confidence to know what to do and who to go to for help and advice. In the words of one student's indicator, 'you trust the school'.

Extra-curricular activities

If we include extra-curricular activities and school trips within this cluster, there would be another hundred indicators to add, seventy-six of them from pupils. These were estimated highly by pupils because:

- 'you develop interest in things you didn't know about before'
- 'you get to know teachers better and get on with them better'
- 'it helps you like school more'
- 'educational trips help you understand your work better and be more interested in it'

Whether all these sub-categories (discipline, counselling, extra-curricular activities) should be included under the heading of 'school climate' is a matter for debate and for individual schools to decide. They may be seen as significant enough to merit a category on their own, particularly if the school were to choose those specific aspects to focus on in self-evaluation.

With that in mind, Table 4.1 separates out responses by different categories and by different group of respondents. In reading across the table to compare responses

Table 4.1 Number of times an indicator was suggested in each category (by group)

	Governors	Parents	Teachers	Pupils	Senior management	Support staff
Climate, ethos (happy, caring, safe)	22	40	35	76	11	22
Good discipline	11	12	19	24	2	3
Counselling, pastoral care	2	6	11	16	6	4
Extra-curricular activities, trips	7	9	3	76	1	4

by different groups, the differing numbers of respondents in each category must be borne in mind.

Climate is often defined as the outward expression of the 'culture' of the school.[1] The word 'culture' in its biological sense describes something that has grown over time and that has invisible, and sometimes deep, roots. In its anthropological sense 'culture' describes a way of seeing and doing things, a set of attitudes to life and accompanying behaviour. Most people in the school-improvement business take school culture as a necessary starting point for development and change. Finding out what the school climate feels like to people in different sectors, and with different experiences of school life, is a useful first step.

Five key features of school climate

- The school is a safe and happy place
- There are places for pupils to go and constructive things to do outside class time
- Pupils and staff behave in a relaxed and orderly way
- Pupils, staff and parents feel that their contribution to the school is valued
- The school is welcoming to visitors and newcomers

RELATIONSHIPS

It is an arbitrary decision to separate relationships from school climate since what makes the climate is, more than anything else, the way people treat and think about each other. A range of relationships may be seen by different groups as characteristic of the good school – pupil–pupil, teacher–pupil, teacher–teacher. Teacher–pupil relationships was the largest category with 139 indicators, 80 from pupils, 23 from parents and governors and 36 from staff.

Most of these descriptors were phrased simply in terms such as 'good relation-ships between teachers and pupils'. Sometimes they were spelt out further – 'good relationships – teachers don't talk down to you', 'teachers take you seriously' and 'teachers treat you as equals (even if you're not really)'. One student suggested as a test of this relationship – 'teachers who recognise and say hello to you in the town and in the street'.

Mutual respect was an explicit criterion mentioned by both teachers and pupils.

There was an interesting difference of emphasis, however. For pupils, this relation-ship was fostered by teachers who were 'accessible', 'approachable' and 'under-standing and helpful'. For teachers, good relationships were helped by pupils who were 'well mannered', 'respectful', 'outgoing', 'responsible' and 'self-motivated'. It says something significant, perhaps, about how young people evaluate their teachers and how their teachers evaluate them. It might offer an interesting theme for discussion within a school and could lead to a deeper understanding of roles and reciprocity, with practical applications for discipline and for resolving conflict.

There were thirty-eight indicators explicitly describing pupil–pupil relation-ships; for example, 'pupils are nice and friendly to each other'. This was a more significant issue than the numbers suggest since it was often implicitly contained in descriptions of school climate and safety. A 'happy' or 'safe' school often, on closer examination, meant a school where there was freedom from fear of other pupils but, more positively, a place where you developed friendships and helped one another.

In some schools particular mention was made of relationships between older and younger pupils. In one secondary school a recurring pupil indicator of the good school was 'older pupils help younger ones'. When feedback on this was given to school management, they were delighted because it was something they had tried to foster within the school. They had created a climate in which older pupils not only helped younger ones with work and study but acted as counsellors and advocates. One member of staff suggested counting the number of times you could see older pupils and younger ones talking or walking together in the playground or corridor as an indicator.

Relationships was a particularly acute issue for support staff, although this dif-fered significantly from school to school. In one school the informal equality of relationships between teachers and support staff was seen as a very positive fea-ture of the school and was consistently cited as an indicator by support staff and teachers alike. In another school, where attitudes were in most other respects posi-tive, there was one sour note – a 'them' and 'us' situation which was a constant source of complaint and friction. This unhappy situation sharpened the perception of what good teaching–support staff relationships should look like:

- teaching staff understand what support staff do
- there is feedback from teaching staff to support staff
- support staff are seen as 'staff', not a separate group
- support staff are given credit for their abilities and competence
- support staff are consulted before changes are made that affect them.

The 'feel' of a school that parents talked about, and often could not quite describe, was very often an outward expression of different and interlocking sets of relation-ships within the school. The language and body language people used were seen as expressions of how people regarded and valued one another. Parents, and other visitors to the school, observed office staff and teachers talking to pupils in the corridors and were more sensitised to those social transactions than the 'insiders'. Typically, a teacher or member of office staff would ask, or instruct, a pupil to show a visitor the way. There are about seven micro-indicators in the following account of a parent's observation of a corridor incident which lasted no more than thirty seconds:

> She asked the lad if he was busy and she waited for his answer like she was asking a real question not a formality. She bent down towards him as if to make herself smaller and touched him on the shoulder. I noticed she called him by his name – Andrew. She asked if he would mind taking the visitor to room thirty-five. She thanked him, in a genuine kind of way as if she was speaking to a friend of her own age.

These micro-incidents are also picked up by new students for whom school is unfamiliar and alive with excitement, but also alive with threat. For the new student, the impact of the first day is so strong that it is one that they often remember for the rest of their lives. It is important, therefore, to tune into their first impressions and to track what happens to these impressions as they accommodate over time. How much is it a projection of an individual anxiety and how much a real feature of the school itself?

Again our dividing lines among categories are flexible and open to debate. We might have divided this section into four categories:

* teacher–pupil relationships
* pupil–pupil relationships
* teacher–teacher relationships
* parent–teacher relationships.

Instead, the first two of these categories provide the basis for this cluster while the last two appear in other clusters – support for teaching, and home–school links. Categorisations such as these are always open to debate and differences of perspective. Any separation of a dynamic whole into discrete parts will always be contested and it is important that people are aware of that and agree on the categories which, for them, provide the most satisfactory framework for their activities.

Since teacher–pupil relationships are seen as the driving force behind so much that happens in the school and classroom, such relationships might take centre stage in school self-evaluation. However, it could be argued with equal force that pupil–pupil relationships are at the heart of the school and that evaluating and getting these right might be a singular focus for school improvement. The research literature would lend weight to the argument from both ethnographic sources and school effectiveness studies.[2]

Ethnographers have been interested in status, roles and pupil cultures, while school effectiveness researchers have concentrated on the relationship between the measurable characteristics of the peer group in relation to school achievement. School improvement is about trying to come at these issues with an action focus – what can the school do to address the issue of pupil–pupil relationships? If the school can involve young people in the evaluation of their relationships, can it involve them to the same degree in taking responsibility for improving them, and doing so in a way that directly enhances achievement?

Five key features of relationships

- There is a shared sense of teamwork among all staff
- Older pupils help younger ones
- Bullying is not tolerated
- Parents and governors feel welcomed and valued in the school
- People address one another in ways which confirm their value as individuals

CLASSROOM CLIMATE

While governors, management and teachers tended to focus on the school as a whole, pupils were more likely to identify indicators relating to what happened in classrooms. There were 117 indicators suggested on classroom climate, 71 of them from pupils. They tended to express this in terms of discrete aspects of the classroom environment, the sum of the parts referring to the ability of the teacher to create and manage a certain kind of climate for learning. In the words of one pupil, 'teachers make a happy atmosphere for people to learn in'.

From a pupil's perspective, an atmosphere 'for people to learn in' can be described in terms of a hierarchy of needs – material, social and psychological – as depicted in Diagram 4.1.

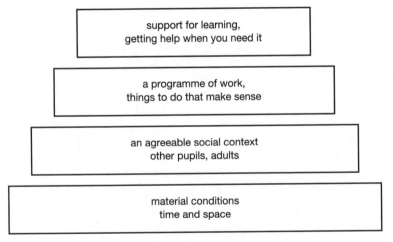

Diagram 4.1 A pupil's hierarchy of needs

Pupils

Pupils' descriptions of the optimum classroom climate fall into these categories in the following way:

Material conditions

- a suitable amount of time for each lesson
- acceptable standards of equipment
- not too many people so you are all crammed up

Social context

- a non-disruptive environment
- no discrimination, or favouritism
- the opportunity to speak and be listened to

A programme of work

- classwork is at your own level of ability
- there is a high standard of work for each lesson
- there is a suitable amount of time to complete and go over work

Support for learning

- teachers walk round the classroom helping children in need
- teachers explain things very clearly and carefully go over topics
- you feel you are achieving something

At the top of this hierarchy is 'support for learning', an issue that received so many mentions we have included it as a separate category.

One pupil had written as an indicator: 'Is there work peace?' It reminded us of the Finnish work for discipline – *tyorauha*, which translates literally as 'work peace'. 'Discipline' in its most positive sense is encapsulated in this description of a good classroom climate.

Having a say in what went on in the classroom was mentioned by pupils of all ages but was especially important for older students. This meant being able to give feedback to the teacher, making suggestions as to how things might be varied or done differently and sharing some of the responsibility for learning and teaching. Allied to this was the importance for students of 'having your opinions listened to and respected'.

Parents

Parents' indicators tended to parallel those of pupils:

- classrooms that are clean and comfortable
- the teacher creates an atmosphere conducive to purposeful work
- the programme of work is geared to individual ability
- the teacher creates and sustains interest in the subject

Teachers

Teachers were less inclined than students to mention aspects of classroom climate but there were twenty-five indicators from teachers about pupil behaviour which might be put into this category because they were seen as making a vital contribution to the atmosphere and sense of purpose in the classroom. Teachers judged classroom climate by students who:

- show a readiness for work
- are self-motivating/self-starters
- are punctual
- have a sense of pride in their work
- have a desire to achieve
- are willing to accept help and advice
- are willing to co-operate with others

Perhaps we ought to have a special category for the characteristics of 'good' pupils to parallel the set of descriptions of the good teacher. When we discussed this idea with a group of senior students, they pointed out the interrelationship of these two things. They were not independent of one another, they said. Good pupils helped to make good teachers just as much as good teachers could make or break pupils. One pupil added this comment: 'It is a two-way thing, but we are used all our lives from junior school on to it being about us – how we should be – be like this, be like that. Why can't you be more like Gloria? But I am Andrea not Gloria.'

It is a reminder that any evaluation of pupil behaviour has to try to understand from the inside, from the pupil perspective, why individuality and difference are so important to them. When this is recognised, it is easier for pupils to accept more generic norms and expectations. The same principle holds true, of course, for teachers. They are also more likely to accept being treated as a group when their individuality has been understood and accommodated.

For the purposes of school self-evaluation, classroom climate may provide a very useful and important category. A school might decide to focus on this area alone and subdivide this into the four different aspects described above. It might add categories such as pupil behaviour and teacher behaviour, to concentrate specifically on what pupils do and what teachers do that creates and inhibits a purposeful and enjoyable climate for both learning and for teaching.

Five key features of classroom climate

- The classroom is a satisfying place to be for pupils and teachers
- There is order, purpose and a relaxed atmosphere in classrooms
- Pupils feel confident in approaching teachers for help
- Pupils work co-operatively and individually as appropriate
- No child is excluded from the possibility of success

SUPPORT FOR LEARNING

Support for learning was the largest category of indicators suggested by pupils. It comprised 206 items which had to do with how they were helped to learn, how they were encouraged and given feedback and ways in which their individual needs and abilities were recognised. Support for learning was seen in the following terms:

- 'teachers want to make it easy for pupils to understand the work'
- 'teachers are aware of the standard you are working at'
- 'you are taught at your own level and ability'
- 'you can go to the teacher for help when you need it'
- 'teachers know how to help someone with a problem'
- 'teachers watch your progress'

Irrespective of whether or not pupils had mentioned support for learning in their personal set of five, none disagreed that it was at the kernel of a good school, nor could we find teachers or parents ready to disagree with that proposition.

Although they might not have included this indicator within their personal set of five, there were few people in other groups who disagreed that support for learning was what characterised the good school.

Behind the words

These indicators suggested by young people may seem at first sight obvious and unremarkable. However, when we took the time to listen to what lay behind the words, they contained some challenging ideas and set high standards. Getting help *when you need it* is a key to effective learning but it is not always easy to meet within the flow of teaching and the demands of classroom life. The challenge to the school is to find ways of meeting that need. Knowing how to help someone with a problem may again seem like an obvious component of a teacher's repertoire, but one insightful group of senior students pointed to the distinct differences among:

- solving a problem for a pupil
- helping the pupil to solve the problem
- helping pupils to solve problems

The demands of the classroom are often met by the quick fix of solving the problem. It takes longer to help pupils work their own way to meaning and longer still to help them develop more generic problem-solving strategies. It is not only a matter of time and pressure; it is a higher-order teaching skill.

The importance of feedback

One secondary student had put a star beside one of his five indicators – 'watching your progress, giving you feedback'. This, he felt, virtually said everything there was to say about support for learning. His teachers were in complete agreement that this was fundamental and, in an ideal world, is what they would all like to achieve. Any evaluation system ought, however, to be able to identify those things which separate the real from the ideal world and help the school as a whole to pay attention to those factors. They were often seen as outwith the control of the individual teacher. Young people themselves have a part to play in that, especially if their own desire for more responsibility and recognition is to be taken seriously. Advances have been made in helping pupils to evaluate their own learning but pupils themselves are usually best placed to know if they have been helped or not and they know the veracity of their response to the teacher's question, 'Do you understand now?'

Self-evaluation which focuses simply on a pupil's satisfaction with a specific piece of work implies that the individual child is his or her own source of learning and motivation. Such a form of self-evaluation stops short of analysing the conditions and context of learning and teaching. How the pupil has been helped to learn is in fact a crucial aspect of his or her evaluation. Whether by the teacher, by other pupils or through other factors in the school and classroom environment, feedback offers to the pupil a more complete understanding of his or her own learning.

It is often their parents who have evidence of a pupil's frustration or confidence in the support they receive because parents are often at the sharp end when their child can't cope with the task set by the teacher. It is at this point that parents are often brought into the discussion on the effectiveness of the school, or the teacher, in supporting learning. Parents who were themselves teachers confessed to being the most rigorous probers of the quality of support that their children got in school.

Five key features of support for learning

- Pupils see themselves as independent learners
- Teachers believe that all pupils can learn and gain success
- The main focus of school is learning
- Learning in and out of school is seen as a coherent whole
- Pupils are involved in reviewing progress, recording achievement and target setting

SUPPORT FOR TEACHING

The emphasis given to support for learning by pupils is paralleled by teachers' emphases on support for teaching. Support for teaching covered all those aspects of the school which helped the teacher to do his or her job effectively. They fell into five categories – sharing and working together (56 indicators), small classes (43), a feeling of being valued (37), resources for teaching and learning (16) and staff development (12). This gave a total of 164 indicators under the 'support for teaching' rubric.

There were marked differences of emphasis between teachers and parents on these issues. Three-quarters of parents' indicators in this category were about small classes whereas for teachers it was only one-fifth. On the other hand, one-third of teacher indicators referred to sharing or collaborative work among staff but for parents it was only one in ten who made such a reference. It highlights two quite distinct sets of issues, social and psychological support on the one hand, and material support on the other. The significance of the first was expressed by a teacher who described the difficulty of 'struggling on as individuals', the psychological support she drew from sharing with colleagues and the practical help that was to be gained by working together on common tasks. It was expressed as 'staff support one another', 'a sense of pulling together', 'people listen to each other' and 'people respect each other's work'. While there were few specific mentions of 'staff development', professional support and development were in fact valued highly by teachers. Whether formal or informal in nature, the chief characteristic of professional support and development was its collegiality, its lateral networking and its ongoing day-to-day character.

Teaching was described by some as a lonely activity in which there was an unequal balance between giving and receiving. It was made easier in a school where that was generally understood and where there were appropriate systems and structures in place: for example, co-operative teaching, learning support and peer mentoring. These were generally the responsibility of the management team and there were strong feelings aired, particularly in secondary schools, about the contribution of management to support for teaching. Feelings, positive and negative, about management and leadership had to do with their:

- accessibility and visibility in the school
- willingness to listen and to act on what they heard
- flexibility and capacity to change
- understanding of, and sympathy for, teachers' needs
- understanding of the needs of pupils
- understanding of the needs of the school as a whole
- valuing of front-line teaching
- strong sense of purpose and direction
- addressing the inequities in staff workload

The last of these was an issue that arose in only some of the schools but confirms findings from other research that it is difficult for teachers to feel supported when they are carrying, or compensating for, their colleagues. In schools where the problem was acute, it was suggested that for management to deny the problem, or to look the other way, simply made matters worse.

It might be argued that many of the issues in the above list have more to do with collegial leadership than with school management. In other words, they spring from a broad educational vision and a shared interest in making that vision work. We have not included 'leadership' indicators within this cluster because there were few references to leadership as such. References were more to the effects and expressions of leadership in the climate and day-to-day life of the school. Some criteria that were suggested also encompassed a wider notion of leadership than the senior management team. Nonetheless, the sensitivity of the management team to the needs of teachers and their private problems is clearly vital.

Structural support – class size

Class size was not frequently included among the top five indicators. It became clear from discussion that it was not necessarily seen as a leading indicator of a good school but was, in certain contexts, a key underpinning of effective learning and teaching. For parents, the issue of class size was seen as important in some contexts and not others. It was much more likely to be mentioned by primary than secondary parents (nineteen inclusions from primary as against four from secondary) but there were differences from school to school. In five of the primary schools it was never mentioned at all but in one school class size was mentioned by eight parents. Its inclusion among the five indicators seemed to depend on the circumstances of the particular school and where class size was clearly inimical to good teaching or effective discipline.

Class size was given only six mentions by pupils (three primary, three secondary). It was mentioned only ten times by teachers (seven primary and three secondary). This was because, in the words of one teacher, it was 'not one of the key quality hallmarks of a good school' but that was not to deny the importance of 'critical mass' in the classroom. The number of people within a given space affected circulation and personal space. It affected: the amount of time a teacher could give to an individual child or group; assessments, record-keeping and the amount and quality of feedback that could be given to any one child; and styles of teaching, pupil relationships, group work and differentiation.

Research findings on class size are equivocal. This may be as much a problem of research design and the lack of any long-term study which has tried to assess the relationship between class size and style of learning and teaching. Evidence from the United States has influenced government policy to reduce class size, particularly in the lower reaches of the primary schools.[3] There is also evidence that teachers of large classes spend more time in preparation.[4]

Our evidence on the importance of class size was what teachers told us about their experience, soundly argued and supported by evidence of day-to-day practice. These views emerged in the context of a highly professional discussion. That is, in the generation and analysis of criteria, teachers spoke positively and reflectively about principles of good practice, putting the learning needs of children at the centre. Only when these were worked down into day-to-day practice was the issue of class size raised and only then did we get to hear about the personal and psychological strain that teachers felt in trying to live up to the high professional standards which they set themselves.

We found this a more convincing body of evidence than the *ex cathedra* pronouncements of policy-makers and some researchers that attainment and class size are not correlated. Our opportunity to work in other countries with much larger class sizes – for example, Thailand and Singapore – exposes the shallow nature of the claim that if it is good enough for them, it is good enough for us. From students' perspectives, it was also clear that class size did influence marking of work, feedback, individual time, physical space and psychological comforts. Teachers' accounts were reinforced independently by those of students who recognised all too clearly the pressures that their teachers were under and the conditions contributing to that.

These findings are paralleled very closely by Neville Bennett's study in which he found consensus among teachers, headteachers, parents and chairs of governors about the adverse effects of large classes on teaching and learning, individual attention and standards of work.[5] A more recent study by Maurice Galton concluded that in smaller classes there is:

- more time spent on task
- more sustained interactions
- more higher-order questioning of pupils
- more feedback on work
- less time spent on routine supervision
- less time spent on exercising control
- less time given over to housekeeping (sorting out papers, handing out books)[6]

This evidence, which reflects the experience of teachers and pupils in our study, will not put the issue beyond dispute, driven as it is by ideological and economic motives. It is convincing, however, to those who know and understand classrooms and who are aware of those factors which lie close to the heart of learning and teaching. A systematic approach to self-evaluation should be able to provide further and still stronger evidence of where, and in what ways, class size counts as a significant factor.

Five key features of support for teaching

- Support for learning and teaching are at the heart of school policies and development planning
- Teachers receive effective support from management
- The size of classes ensures that all teachers can teach effectively
- Teachers share successes and problems with one another
- Parents are seen as partners in pupils' learning

TIME AND RESOURCES

This cluster of indicators is concerned with the school building as a resource, access to, and use of, what it contains. Time has also fallen into this cluster because, in the minds of pupils, it was closely associated with the use of resources and, in the discussion among teachers, it was described as a diminishing resource which deeply affected the quality of school life. Monitoring how resources were used could, it was suggested, be taken together with the monitoring of how time was 'spent'.

There were 136 indicators suggested which had to do with resources. Ninety-three of these came from young people. One-third of these were from primary school pupils describing things to use and places to go – games and sports equipment, musical instruments, computers, libraries with lots of books, and safe places. The emphasis among secondary students was more on the access to resources and access for specific groups in particular: for example, pupils who were disabled or who had special needs.

Privileged access – for example, by teachers or by certain students only – was resented. For those eager to learn, there was frustration that there was so much 'down time' during the school day. It is interesting that so many of these references were to educational resources, things that schools contained but to which access was limited. Twenty of the indicators (eight from secondary students, seven from primary pupils and three from support staff) had more to do with the school as a social place. They were concerned about places to go at break times, before and after school, and the value of common rooms or other comfortable, purpose-built areas in which they could sit, talk or listen to music.

In some cases the only spaces pupils could lay claim to were the cloakroom areas and toilets. These areas could then become the focus for the 'under-life' of the school; in sociological language a 'behaviour setting' where different norms and standards of behaviour were allowed to operate. The school culture and the 'toilet culture' did not always sit easily side by side. Some pupils saw the neglect of their toilets as symbolic of their status in the school. The issues were of privacy, dignity and, most fundamentally, safety. 'Do the toilet doors have locks on them?' was one suggested indicator. Toilets were often avoided because they were not seen as 'safe places'. Although parents did not include toilets in their priority list, when we raised the issue with them they were quick to acknowledge the importance of this and they frequently expressed concern at their children coming home and heading straight for the toilet because they were unwilling to use the school facilities.

Pupils were more likely than any other group to emphasise the physical aspects of the school, its cleanliness or lack of litter, its ergonomic features, its entrances and exits, its forbidden places. Their concerns about graffiti and litter, their welcome for fresh paint and carpets and decent accommodation were all reflections of their status as users of the building and their sense of identification with the school as a place for them.

There was relatively little mention of resources by teachers (a total of sixteen indicators). This did not mean that resources were seen as inconsequential but rather they were not the most significant determining quality of a good school. Those who did emphasise resources did so because to have them opened up a range of options for pupils and teachers in terms of time, organisation and effectiveness of learning.

Time

For teachers, the most significant resource issue was that of time. Although it did not figure in teachers' lists of indicators, it quickly rose to the surface as an issue as soon as discussion was opened up. Time, said one teacher, 'is the issue of the nineties'. Taking time and 'making' time was, for staff at all levels, a major issue and seen as one of the strongest determinants of school climate, staff morale and ultimately of school quality and effectiveness.

For teachers, the issue is having time for things that matter: learning and teaching. Whatever could be seen as supporting these was valued, whether that was review or development planning. They were seen as 'wasting' time to the extent that there was no discernible link to classroom or to wider school learning.

Time has a life of its own. It is a limited commodity. So how do you 'make' time?

asked one teacher. The answer was that 'you borrow from your domestic and family life – and never get round to paying it back. Or you take it from students.'

A teacher, described by her head as a first-class, committed teacher, admitted to her changing relationship with her students through lack of time for that relationship.

> I know perfectly well I am not as good with them as I used to be. I am short with them. I sometimes treat them quite badly and I always go home feeling bad about it myself. I just feel sometimes I don't have the breathing space and they are crowding in on me. It is wrong, absolutely wrong, that they should suffer for that.

Pupils were sensitive to when time was being taken from them but also perceptive about pressure on their teachers. They appeared less concerned about the quantity of time given to them by teachers than the quality of time – the quality of attention, quality of listening and the implicit quality of concern. 'Being there for you' was an expression used by some older secondary students.

Five key features of use of time and resources

- Organisation of classes is conducive to all pupils learning effectively
- Deployment of resources is the result of a shared, negotiated approach
- Time for teachers to plan, assess and develop professionally is well used
- Resources are available to pupils within and outwith the school day
- The school is a community resource

ORGANISATION AND COMMUNICATION

Everyone wants a well-organised school. It is, as one chair of governors pointed out, a tautology to say that an organisation should be well organised, but what are the characteristics of a good organisation? How would you know one when you saw it? It was not hard to tell when good organisation and communication were missing, it was suggested, because it manifested itself in friction, mishap, mistakes and low morale. What, asked the chair of one governing body, are the features of this school's organisation and communication that we would wish to be measured by?

There were ninety-one indicators in all which tried to answer that question, suggesting some of the things that make for a good organisation and effective communication. Although these can be separated into two categories, they were generally seen as inextricably linked. Twenty-one of the indicators came from governors, fifteen from senior management, twenty-nine from teachers and three from pupils. The nine indicators suggested by parents were all to do with home–school communications and relationships and have been dealt with under that heading.

Given the relatively small representation from governors and senior management, it is a further illustration of how different groups have different priorities and perspectives. There were also quite different ways of looking at the organisation. Governors were more likely to see it from the top down, pupils from the bottom up and teachers from the middle upwards and downwards.

Governors were most likely to mention leadership, strong direction from the head, clear structure and lines of communications within the school as key features. They placed equal emphasis on the school's relationship with the local and wider community and with parents and employers. The responsiveness of the school to what was happening in the world outside was seen from a governor's standpoint as particularly significant. The good organisation was, in their view, one which was receptive and adaptable to change from the outside but which had a clear sense of its own stance and values. It had a capacity to manage the effects of change on the internal environment. In other words, management was able to take teachers along with them.

There were eight indicators identifying adaptability to change as the hallmark of an effective school. The following are three of them, one from a governor, two from senior management, who defined indicators in this area:

- Is there a balance between change and opportunity on the one hand, stability and time for thought and evaluation on the other?
- Is communication open enough so that everyone feels able to come up with suggestions for change and development without criticism?
- How welcome are new ideas and new ways of doing things?

At a more basic level, one secondary school governor suggested that an effective organisation could be measured specifically by examining movement around the school. On the quantitative side, time saved and time wasted could be measured. On the qualitative side, the orderliness and the purpose with which teachers and students went about their business would, he suggested, tell you a great deal. You could be sure, someone else added, that underpinning such orderly movement would be a sound system of communication.

Teachers' litmus tests of the organisation were more concerned with teacher time, movement and information. Good organisation and communication were measured by teachers knowing where they were going, both physically and metaphorically, and having the time and opportunity to give to their main priority – teaching. Good organisation was created by management and tested in the behaviour of pupils.

The 'level-headed' school

One member of the teaching staff had as one of her criteria 'a calm, level-headed school'. Asked to explain the meaning and importance of that she described her school as one in which students were reasonable people because staff dealt with things in a reasonable, sensible and low-key way. Staff did not become agitated and over-excited, did not 'raise their blood pressure over trivia', did not heighten the tension level and did not allow *their* problems to spill over into corridors and classrooms. In her words, the calm, level-headed school is one in which:

- there are clearly understood ways of doing things
- there is good communication
- people talk about their jobs
- issues are dealt with promptly and not allowed to fester
- people feel, and are, accountable to one another
- things are sorted out informally
- people work at their relationships
- there is consistency in what is expected
- time is made for things that are important

Although only three pupils proposed indicators specifically to do with effective organisation, it was a subject on which they usually had views. These are perhaps best summarised by one student's explanation of his indicator, 'everyone is given an equal chance to prove themselves and find out their niche':

> A good school works because everyone has something to take responsibility for, not just teachers. Pupils can take responsibility for a lot of things that would make the school run better. It prepares you for later life. It doesn't think that what teachers teach you in class is what you learn. You learn by being given opportunities to do things and take decisions. The best thing about this school is that everyone is given a chance to prove themself and find out their niche.

Five key feature of organisation and communication

- School decision-making is an open, participatory process
- The views of all within the school are listened to
- Pupils have forums for discussing their concerns and problems
- Parents and governors are well informed about school policies and practice
- The community has a strong, positive view of the school

EQUITY

There were ninety-seven indicators which had to do with fair and equal treatment, to democracy and pupils being given opportunities to influence what happened to them and others in the school. Sixty-seven of those indicators came from pupils, twelve from teachers, four from parents and four from governors. A summarising indicator for all these issues was suggested by a member of senior management: 'How strong is the equal opportunities culture?'

A number of specific ways in which the strength of that culture might be measured is offered by different groups. The ideas can be placed into four categories:

1 The school as a place for everyone

In two inner-city primary schools the following indicators were suggested by children: 'having disabled children in your class', 'a school which has deaf children', '[a school] where there are people who are all different'. There were eleven other references by children to a good school being one which welcomed *all* children from different backgrounds and with different abilities and disabilities. These suggestions all came from schools which had made special efforts to accommodate physically disabled children and children with a range of special needs. It was not an indicator that appeared in the lists from any other school, and, indeed, there was some concern expressed by parents in one of those schools that the attention and resources for children with special needs might mean less time given to their own child. In schools where celebration of diversity was an integral aspect of the school culture it was widely accepted that the value that this added to the school community was significant, enhancing children's social awareness and view of the world.

2 Opportunities for participation in the life of the school

Some schools made special efforts to take a step beyond the accommodation of children with special needs by giving them roles and responsibilities within the classroom and the school on a par with other children. In primary schools these included tasks such as giving out books, answering the telephone, running the tuck shop, banking the money, setting out the assembly hall and showing visitors round the school. In secondary schools there was a variety of roles as prefects, mentors, members of the school council or team captains, and opportunities to organise events, trips and projects, or to chair group discussions.

In one primary school we were shown around by two children, a girl and a boy. Neither was from Year 6, nor did this job as a matter of course. The boy had hearing and speech difficulties. For the purposes of a tour guide, it may not have been the ideal choice but it carried a strong message to us as visitors as well as to everyone within the school community. It was a clear signal of self-worth to the individual child too. Discussing with the teacher afterwards how she came to choose the two children as tour guides, it was clear that it had been a finely balanced decision, with the various purposes and functions served being carefully weighed. The fact that this was a multi-racial classroom with fifteen different ethnic backgrounds represented was a further factor in the teacher's decision-making. The critics who parody political correctness have either never experienced such decision-making or are unaware of how such apparently trivial decisions can affect the sense of identity and self-esteem of small children. Children themselves were acutely aware of it and the more articulate were able to express it for our benefit.

3 Attitudes to difference and individuality

Children both wished to be recognised as individuals and 'treated the same'. Some children and young people said that they did not like attention being drawn to their differences and resented special allowances being made for them. With regard to homework, for example, being exempted from homework or being given less to do was often seen as a slight. Some young people in secondary schools commented on their teachers' good intentions but felt that they were being 'overcared for' or patronised by being given special work. Some felt equally diminished in the eyes of their peers when allowances were made for their 'home circumstances'.

To be accepted as one of the group it was felt that teachers should make more of your commonalities than your differences. However, it seems to us significant, although we have no more than impressionistic evidence to substantiate this, that there was less sensitivity to 'being different' in schools where value was placed on the 'differentness' and individuality of people. In other words, in a strong equal opportunities culture, there is less of a perceived need to conform to a narrow range of norms, hand in hand with a deeper shared understanding of what diversity means.

4 Action to deal with racism, sexism or other forms of discrimination

Ultimately the most telling indicator of the strong equal opportunities culture was what happened in response to discrimination, racial and sexual harassment or bullying. Young people and parents spoke about the importance for them of having faith that something would be done in response to a complaint. Reporting back to the child or parent by a member of staff on what had been done, or not done, was also valued highly.

However, much of what was seen by pupils as unfairness and discrimination (a word they rarely used) was less likely to take the form of a single incident and was often difficult to pin down or define. It was sometimes embedded in language, register, tone and form of address, jokes and nicknames used by pupils or by staff. The most insidious form of discrimination was expressed in attitudes and behaviour for which pupils could not always find descriptive words. Being ignored by a teacher or being treated, in the eyes of the young person, as not worth spending time on conveyed messages to pupils about their own self-worth. 'She doesn't have time for you' was normally said in a figurative, not in a literal, sense. Pupils recognised and made allowances for overworked teachers who could not find the time they would have liked to give. Teachers pointed out in the course of discussions that pupils who felt insecure or vulnerable were those most likely to be hurt by teachers appearing to treat them as unimportant.

It was difficult for pupils to know what they could do about those subtler, longer-term forms of discrimination. The opportunity to give feedback in anonymous form, either directly to the individual teacher, or in some more generalised way, was seen as a most useful option. It is perhaps expressed best by what one nine-year-old wrote: 'I would like people to say what they think about the way they are treated and for people to try to treat them better.'

Five key features of equity

- Pupils have faith in school's policy on equal opportunities
- Cultural, moral, intellectual and social diversity is seen as adding value to school life and learning
- All staff believe they have a part to play in promoting an equal opportunity culture

- The planning and organisations of the curriculum takes account of the needs of all pupils
- All pupils have opportunities to take responsibility in the classroom, school and extra-curricular activities

RECOGNITION OF ACHIEVEMENT

We had difficulty in finding a name for this cluster of items because the descriptors offered were not directly about achievement as an indicator but about those things which promoted, recognised and celebrated achievement. There were 91 indicators in total, falling into three main categories – setting high standards (42), having high expectations (19) and recognising achievement with incentives and awards (27); a further 7 indicators referred to the importance of having individual targets, and 6 made reference to 'added value'.

In this category 31 of the indicators came from pupils, 34 from teachers, 19 from governors, 10 from senior management and 6 from parents. Given the number involved, this represents a much stronger emphasis from management than from teachers, pupils and parents. Follow-up discussion allowed us to gauge the degree to which the words meant the same to different groups.

Those discussions revealed that achievement was being spoken about in two quite distinct ways – in terms of the individual pupil and in terms of the school's external profile. There was a significant widespread agreement that a central purpose of the school was to help all children achieve and, without undermining basic skills, to broaden the definition of achievement. Most of the schools we visited had some form of awards for effort or diligence, attendance improvement, or particular contributions to the school. These were accompanied by concerted efforts to push young people over critical thresholds, for example from D into the A–C band at GCSE level.

One governor's meeting in a secondary school began with the assertion that it was all about 'bums on seats', and the chair regretted that the push to demonstrate achievement had skewed resources and teacher time away from a broader and deeper approach. An unprompted discussion among Year 10 students in one school centred on the issue of whether the school was still as committed as it once was to individual achievement. 'I used to feel that this school cared about how well I was doing. Now I just think the only thing it cares about it is how well *it's* doing.' This Year 9 student expressed a view that struck a chord with others in her group. They felt that the balance of caring had swung too far towards caring what outsiders thought, or, as one student put it, 'what the school *thinks* people outside want it to be'.

In this school it was also a concern of staff who worried about the school increasing its popularity and expanding beyond its optimum capacity in both a physical and social sense. In a physical sense it meant less space. In a psychological sense the diminishing of personal space led to greater friction, visible in what one member of staff described as the new phenomenon of 'corridor madness'. There was an apprehension that the school, in its pursuit of numbers and status, might lose its caring atmosphere both with regard to staff and in respect of the individual student.

The dangers of 'the popular school' was a recurring theme in different groups. How could the school maintain the individual concern and caring for the success of individual students in its striving to meet external attainment criteria?

There will continue to be, in the foreseeable future, both a political and educational imperative to include specific attainment measures such as National Curriculum tests and GCSEs at the centre of school self-evaluation. These are important proxies for a school's effectiveness and its accountability, but in no school did we find a belief that they told the story of the school's quality of purpose. Teachers will continue to be unhappy with such measures if they are not more broadly defined, set in a wider context and accompanied by health warnings. It may be some time before policy-makers come up with a more satisfactory set of measures, but schools should neither hold their breath nor simply bemoan the inadequacy of the data. They can find and demonstrate ways of recognising achievement in its widest sense. What we might call the school's 'ethos of achievement' describes what the school really values, how it prioritises its efforts and its time and what it recognises as worthwhile success. It is best measured by the perceptive insights and ongoing systematic evaluation of those who live within that ethos day by day. The more schools play a proactive part in this, the more likely it is that public perception will broaden and that policy-makers will raise their sights.

Five key features of recognition of achievement

- There is a climate of achievement in the school
- All pupils have an equal chance of having their achievements recognised
- Reward rather than punishment is the prevailing approach throughout the school
- There is consensus in the school about what constitutes 'success'
- Staff achievements are recognised and rewarded

HOME–SCHOOL LINKS

There were 103 indicators concerned with links between home and school, and between parents and teachers. These break down into three main categories – parents feeling a part of the school (43), good relationships between parents and teachers (39) and keeping parents informed (19); there were 4 references by parents to getting feedback on pupil progress. Of the 103 indicators, 49 were suggested by parents and 19 came from governors; 15 indicators came from teachers, 9 from senior management, 7 from support staff and 4 from pupils.

For the parent, the first reading of the school is in terms of how he or she is treated. Who receives them when they walk through the door and does it convey a genuine warmth of welcome? How long are they kept waiting? If they are waiting, are they given an explanation? Do they get to see who they want to see or are they fobbed off with someone else? In our own visits to ten schools the quality of the reception we received gave us an insight into what parents or other outsiders might learn on their first visit. In one school we were met by two girls at the front door. They greeted us by name and knew why we had come. They told us that the head was expecting us and had a coffee waiting for us. They gave us a little background to the school on the way to her office.

A teacher had offered as an indicator 'Are parents behind the school?', adding in follow-up discussion, 'You get nowhere if parents aren't behind the school, wanting the best from it for their children and the best for it as a school.' This was endorsed from a parental perspective. Although parents who took part in this study could not be regarded as a representative sample, those who did participate were clear that for them at least there were strong and specific benefits from close co-operation between home and school. Some of these were described as:

- knowing where the school as a whole was going
- being reassured that their child was given the fullest opportunities to learn
- finding out how they could help their child at home
- being reassured that their child was fitting in and making friends
- being alerted quickly to problems, either in learning or behaviour
- keeping open a channel of communication on a regular basis

Mechanisms such as a home–school diary or primary learning record were mentioned by parents as helping them to keep in touch with their child's life in the classroom and helping to maintain a dialogue with their children's teachers. Home links or community liaison teachers were also specifically mentioned as having helped to build those bridges between home and school. In two schools, our sessions with parents were conducted with translators present, demonstrating the importance of these otherwise silent voices being heard in school consultation and decision-making.

There were also some strong feelings expressed by parents on the subject of bullying and racial harassment. They felt that these issues could not be tackled unless there were strong supportive links between home and school, and regular communication and agreement on how the bullies and the bullied should be dealt with. It was a discussion which touched on one of the more sensitive areas of home, school and community relationships, and conflict of values. It illustrated again that parents come to issues such as this with a different perspective and different proposed remedies.

In some cases this is because they are uninformed about what the school is doing and can gain a lot from information or training sessions which put the issue into a broader context. In some cases it is because the school has, in the past, been oblivious to factors in home and community and even to what was happening within the school itself. Often things that happened in school were passed by children into the parent/community intelligence network without these things coming to light within the school itself. It is salutary to be reminded that a decade or so ago many schools denied or underestimated the existence of bullying and racial or sexual harassment within the school, while pupils and parents were fully aware of what was really happening.

Schools which have done in-depth work with parents, through interviews, home visits or parent workshops, have learned a lot they never knew, not only about home and community life but about the hidden life of the school and classrooms.

Five key features of home–school links

- Parents play an active part in their children's learning
- Parents are confident that problems will be dealt with and feedback given
- The school provides for the social, cultural and linguistic backgrounds of pupils
- Parent–teacher meetings are useful and productive
- Pupil progress is monitored and shared with parents on a regular basis

SUMMARY

This chapter has looked more closely at the ten themes within which specific indicators have been defined. We have, as far as possible, tried to remain faithful to what we were given and, wherever possible, to retain the language and essential ideas of those who suggested them. If at times the indicators look all too familiar, that may be because there is a constituency of ideas which has been shaped by school discourse, the literature and the media as well as by people's own individual experiences of school. As participants in the process, we felt that in most cases we were being offered more than words: deeply held feelings and beliefs about school. We believe, therefore, that these indicators are real and not merely ideological rhetoric. In many respects they are in the mainstream of thinking about good schools and the welfare of children, but they also offer a strong challenge to 'common sense', ideology and research wisdom.

5

THE GOOD TEACHER

'Ambassadors of society to the kingdom of the child' is how Sir Percy Nunn described teachers some eighty years ago. For the last twenty years, school effectiveness researchers have been edging closer to the discovery that the single most important ingredient of the good school is the good teacher. It was clear from our study that teachers have an intuitive or studied understanding that they have much to learn from children and that there is also much that children can teach them. The subjective evidence from pupils has also provided a stimulus for many teachers to explore more general research findings which provide a rich and useful body of literature on the subject.[1]

The Canadian researcher Peter Coleman argues that the best sources of evidence on good teachers are pupils.[2] This view might be contested by other researchers who have brought a sophistication of insight into what teachers do and have written insightfully on the subject. There is now an extensive literature on the subject,[3] but however good the objective observation, it has to be taken together with the subjective, introspective evidence of those who live day to day with teachers and see them in their darkest, as well as their brightest, periods.

In our discussions with pupils we followed up their indicators of a good school with questions about what makes for good teaching and good teachers. In primary schools we asked pupils to think of a teacher whom they thought was really good and to describe that person's behaviour and qualities.

These descriptions tended to refer to three different kinds of attribute – personal qualities, interpersonal skills and professional characteristics. Personal qualities included kindness, generosity of spirit, honesty and humour – attributes which are hard to learn or to teach but perhaps are all the more important for that. The second category contained a group of skills that could be acquired or embellished: for example, listening, not shouting, keeping confidences, emphasising the positive. In the category 'professional characteristics' we included those things which student teachers go to college to learn – explaining things, noticing when you are stuck, helping you to understand, helping you to like what teachers are teaching.

Asked to think about a good teacher they had, and come up with a description of that person, pupils were able quickly and spontaneously to generate lists and clusters of characteristics. The following list was composed by a group of Year 8 girls. It was acknowledged generally by teachers in that school as fair and insightful and as offering a good checklist for self-evaluation.

The good teacher

- is kind
- is generous
- listens to you
- encourages you
- has faith in you
- keeps confidences
- likes teaching children
- likes teaching their subject
- helps you like their subject
- takes time to explain things
- helps you when you're stuck
- tells you how you are doing
- allows you to have your say
- makes sure you understand
- helps people who are slow
- doesn't give up on you
- cares for your opinion
- makes you feel clever
- treats people equally
- stands up for you
- makes allowances
- tells the truth
- is forgiving

One teacher suggested the list should be put up on the classroom wall as a reference point for both the teacher and her students. Another agreed to do this once they had gone through a similar exercise for the good student. With two such lists side by side on the classroom wall it was much easier for the teacher to hold her students to account as well as being reminded by them when she was not meeting expectations. Good teachers and good students do not exist in some kind of idealised vacuum. They are a product of one another's expectations and behaviour. In the language of biology their relationship is 'symbiotic'.

The list of qualities was described by one teacher as the 'Mother Teresa Charter', perhaps referring to those saintly qualities which, for anyone, would be an unrealistic counsel of perfection. There is a 'super-human' quality in this that exceeds the norms of everyday relationships. Having a transparent commitment to helping others and being able to sustain that on a daily basis could not be expected of many teachers. But young people themselves did not look for or expect saintly teachers. They also live in the real world and spoke as generously about their teachers as they would about friends or family who often let them down. Good teachers were good teachers whatever the context they worked in or whatever the pressures they were under. The essential quality was expressed by some as 'being there for you'. This was particularly true for vulnerable young people experiencing difficulties at home or school. Their highest praise was reserved for teachers who 'have faith in you', 'make you feel clever' and 'really care for your opinion'.

If there is in this an overemphasis on the 'soft' interpersonal qualities of the teacher, it in no way undermines the importance of the 'strong' qualities – having high expectations, motivating and challenging young people to do better. One young person spoke about being 'overcared for' to the extent that her educational needs were being forgotten. Although she had difficulties at home and a turbulent emotional history, she wanted to be given homework, to be treated like others and have demands made of her. She wanted to be encouraged to succeed.

THE VIRTUES OF STRICT TEACHERS

These discussions were helpful in getting a deeper understanding of what young people really meant when they talked about 'kind', 'bossy' or 'strict' teachers. One group of eleven–twelve-year-olds explained why they liked strict teachers. They distinguished between teachers who are 'strict for you' and 'strict for themselves'. As the lists below illustrate, the essential difference was that the strictness had a purpose they could understand and they would, sooner or later, be grateful to that teacher for being so hard on them.

Strict for you	**Strict for themselves**
• make you do it and do it well	• make you do it
• you do it because you know they care for you	• make you do it because they say so
• you respect them but you're not frightened	• it is strict for its own sake
• you don't want to disappoint them	• it is to control you not help you
• you learn a lot more	• it is to make up for their own disorganisation
• you make good progress	• it makes a tense atmosphere
	• you don't learn so well

These insights have a depth and spontaneity which are much more difficult to find from the perspective of an 'objective' observer in the school or classroom. They bring new knowledge as well as being powerfully reinforcing of existing knowledge and they shed new light on 'high expectations' and 'the self-fulfilling prophecy', and help move these from purely theoretical insights to practical application. They have resonance not only with teachers but with parents who said that they have come to a better understanding of their relationship with their children and the fine balance between authority and control, permissiveness and permission.

Younger children have fewer words to use and less complex constructions to express their feelings, but they were equally clear about teachers they found helpful and those they did not. The following is a list composed by a Year 2/3 class.

The good teacher

- is very clever
- doesn't shout
- helps you every day

- is not bossy
- has faith in you
- is funny
- is patient
- is good at work
- tells you clearly what to do
- helps you with mistakes
- marks your work
- helps you to read
- helps you with spelling
- has got courage

EXPECTATIONS GO BOTH WAYS

There is much exhortation in schools on how to behave properly and how to meet expectations that adults have of you, yet, as one girl put it, 'expectations go both ways'. A group of students who embarked on a discussion of this theme came to the conclusion that there should be greater equality and reciprocity in the teacher/ student relationship. They pointed out a lack of consistency across the school in what was expected of students and what was expected of teachers. Some teachers were apparently allowed to breach those standards which were set for them as young women. This is illustrated in the following list where a group of Year 8 girls described standards of dress and behaviour in their school.

What they expect of you	**What they do**
• dress smartly	• dress sloppily
• be polite/show respect	• put you down/speak rudely to you
• talk quietly	• shout at you
• don't bully weaker people	• pick on people/call them names
• apologise/say you're sorry	• never apologise
• treat people equally	• play favourites

A SPIRAL OF TROUBLE

The need for good discipline was common to young people of all ages. We did not find anyone who did not welcome that. Discussions about what constitutes discipline were illuminating. Primary pupils and secondary students recognised ways in which good teachers avoided trouble and diffused conflict. They also recognised when good teachers were under stress and broke their own rules. They were able to accommodate and make allowances for that. But they also recognised how trouble could escalate. Diagram 5.1, which was offered by a thirteen-year-old student, depicts what she called a 'spiral of trouble'. The spiral described:

- how you get into trouble and how you can't get out
- why it happens and how it could be prevented

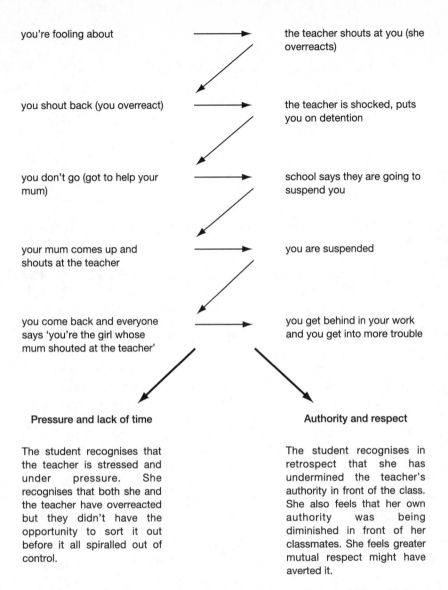

you're fooling about → the teacher shouts at you (she overreacts)

you shout back (you overreact) → the teacher is shocked, puts you on detention

you don't go (got to help your mum) → school says they are going to suspend you

your mum comes up and shouts at the teacher → you are suspended

you come back and everyone says 'you're the girl whose mum shouted at the teacher' → you get behind in your work and you get into more trouble

Pressure and lack of time

The student recognises that the teacher is stressed and under pressure. She recognises that both she and the teacher have overreacted but they didn't have the opportunity to sort it out before it all spiralled out of control.

Authority and respect

The student recognises in retrospect that she has undermined the teacher's authority in front of the class. She also feels that her own authority was being diminished in front of her classmates. She feels greater mutual respect might have averted it.

Diagram 5.1 A thirteen-year-old student's description of a 'spiral of trouble'

This capacity to reflect on, and analyse, events with a degree of objectivity offers to the school a source which it can use. It begins to offer a structure for self-evaluation as well. Critical incident analysis is widely used as a technique in research and staff development. Everyone within the school community would be able to furnish at least one 'critical' incident on which much of school or classroom life turned. Analysing and discussing these incidents in the classroom can be a positive and illuminating experience and can be used to identify points at which intervention can occur to stop the spiral of trouble dead in its tracks. It brings home forcefully the options that teachers and pupils have at their disposal to do things differently and to determine their own futures.

6

INSPECTION PRIORITIES

Are they yours?

The Office of Standards in Education refers to a list of published criteria for school review.[1] Twenty-three of these were put on to individual cards and used as a basis for group discussion in the partnership schools.

Groups were asked to select from the twenty-three cards the five most important and the three least important as they saw it. Having each indicator on a single card allowed people physically to lift and rearrange cards as a way of expressing their view. This defocusing away from face-to-face discussion allowed the more inhibited and less articulate to participate and to think aloud in a more spontaneous and reflective, and less formal, way.

Most of the cards represented important aspects of school life and most groups found it difficult to choose only five. The discussion which took place in the selection of the cards and in the comparison and questioning between groups afterwards was usually animated and informative. It touched on values and experiences important to people from a learning and teaching perspective. Across all groups there were some cards which were consistently chosen and some consistently rejected. Table 6.1 shows the twenty-three cards.

Diagram 6.1 shows the top ten cards chosen across all groups.

The ten lowest rated cards chosen are shown in Diagram 6.2.

These overall figures illustrate clear preferences across all groups but mask differences between groups. Tables 6.2 to 6.6 give the top five priorities group by group. For purposes of easier comparison, we have also weighted the responses to take account of group size and to give an index of importance for that group. Weighting is done simply by taking any single selection of a card as a percentage of all selections by that group. So in the case of governors, for example, where there were thirteen groups who made selections, a card appearing thirteen times would have a 100 per cent score. The best achieved was in fact a six out of thirteen, a score of 46 per cent. These figures are not number of times selected but percentage of times selected within the total number of selections made by that group.

These tables illustrate once again the solid common core of agreement as well as highlighting those issues which are from one particular perspective. How do we explain such a high level of agreement about priorities in ten very different schools from Canterbury to Newcastle, with disparate and random groups of students, staff, parents and governors? Or is such a finding obvious and unsurprising?

Table 6.1 Twenty-three card sort items

PUPILS BEHAVE WELL IN AND AROUND THE SCHOOL	STAFF HAVE A GOOD UNDERSTANDING OF THE NEEDS OF PUPILS	PUPILS WITH SPECIAL NEEDS ACHIEVE TARGETS SET IN THEIR INDIVIDUAL PLAN	MORAL PRINCIPLES SUCH AS JUSTICE ARE PROMOTED	PUPIL PROGRESS IS MONITORED AND FEEDBACK GIVEN
PUPILS ARE ENCOURAGED TO TAKE RESPONSIBILITY AND SHOW INITIATIVE	ROLES OF SENIOR MANAGEMENT, GOVERNORS AND STAFF ARE CLEARLY UNDERSTOOD	THE CURRICULUM COMPLIES WITH NATIONAL GUIDELINES	CLASSES ARE WELL MANAGED	THE STANDARD OF PUPILS' WORK IS CHALLENGING
COLLECTIVE WORSHIP TAKES PLACE	THE SCHOOL HAS A GOOD RELATIONSHIP WITH THE WIDER COMMUNITY	REGULAR ASSESSMENT IS CARRIED OUT	STAFF HAVE A SECURE UNDERSTANDING OF THEIR SUBJECT	THERE ARE STRONG HOME–SCHOOL LINKS
THE SCHOOL PROMOTES HEALTHY LIVING	PUPILS ACHIEVE OR DO BETTER THAN KEY STAGE TARGETS	THE CURRICULUM MEETS THE NEEDS OF ALL PUPILS	THE SCHOOL IS A SAFE PLACE FOR PUPILS	THERE ARE HIGH EXPECTATIONS OF ALL PUPILS
STAFF WORK CO-OPERATIVELY TOWARDS SHARED GOALS	RESOURCES ARE USED EFFICIENTLY AND EFFECTIVELY	STAFF DEVELOPMENT IS MOTIVATING FOR STAFF		

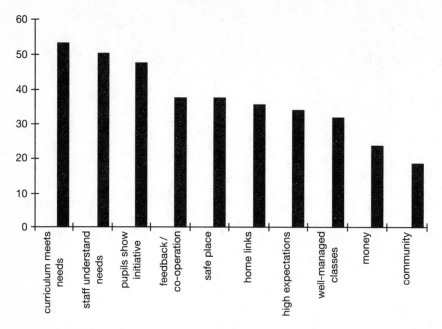

Diagram 6.1 Total number of times a card was included in the top five in all groups

In fact it was surprising for the schools and surprising for the project team. This may be because conventional wisdom considerably overestimates the differences between what parents want and what teachers want, or between pupils' and teachers' priorities. This data suggests that there is a core of values which are widely agreed and that where there are differences it is more a matter of emphasis and perspective than conflict.

To some extent, this difference in emphasis by different groups may have to do with language. 'Classes well managed', 'understanding needs', 'school is a safe place' and 'roles of senior management' which have different resonances for

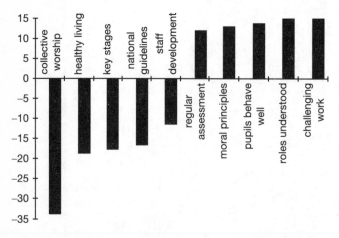

Diagram 6.2 Total number of times a card was included in the bottom three in all groups

Table 6.2 Top five priorities, parents

Priority	Index of priority
Staff have a good understanding of the needs of pupils	55
The curriculum meets the needs of all pupils	50
There are strong home–school links	50
Pupils are encouraged to take responsibility and show initiative	45
The school is a safe place for pupils	45

Table 6.3 Top five priorities, teachers

Priority	Index of priority
Staff work collaboratively towards shared goals	80
The curriculum meets the needs of all pupils	74
Staff have a good understanding of the needs of pupils	50
Pupils are encouraged to take responsibility and show initiative	50
There are high expectations of all pupils	45

Table 6.4 Top five priorities, governors

Priority	Index of priority
The curriculum meets the needs of all pupils	46
Pupil progress is monitored and feedback given	46
Staff have a good understanding of the needs of pupils	40
Pupils are encouraged to take responsibility and show initiative	25
There are strong home–school links	20

Table 6.5 Top five priorities, pupils/students

Priority	Index of priority
Staff have a good understanding of the needs of pupils	70
The curriculum meets the needs of all pupils	65
The school is a safe place for pupils	60
Pupils are encouraged to take responsibility and show initiative	55
Pupils with special needs achieve targets in their individual work plan	45

Table 6.6 Top five priorities, senior management

Priority	Index of priority
Staff work collaboratively towards shared goals	80
The curriculum meets the needs of all pupils	60
Staff have a good understanding of the needs of pupils	55
Pupils are encouraged to take responsibility and show initiative	55
There are strong home–school links	55

different stakeholders, and the perceptions which lie behind the words, are significant in shaping priorities. Words contain images and ideas which could be
explored and explained through the card sort activity. Whether it was students,
teachers or parents, the group always seemed to look for bigger concepts. They
tended to choose cards which reflected deeper values. 'Pupils behave well in and
around the school' tended to be rejected in favour of 'pupils are encouraged to take
responsibility and show initiative'. 'Pupil progress is monitored and feedback
given' seemed to be interpreted as a higher principle than 'regular assessment is
carried out'.

It was all the more important for us, therefore, to tune into the negotiation process during the card sort and, in debriefing the exercise, to try to understand
people's thinking. A separate volume could be written about each of the twenty-
three cards but we have restricted ourselves to dealing with just a few that help to
illuminate how different groups were thinking about what school is for. We have
shown the index referred to earlier under each priority.

Staff have a good understanding of the needs of pupils

- governors 46
- parents 55
- pupils 70
- teachers 50
- senior management 46

The curriculum meets the needs of all pupils

- governors 46
- parents 50
- pupils 65
- teachers 74
- senior management 60

These two cards were commonly selected across all groups and valued more or less
equally. Both were about pupil needs and in a sense represented two sides of the
same coin. The first emphasised staff understanding, the second referred to the
curriculum meeting the needs of all pupils. Some groups either chose both of these
cards and laid them side by side, or even stapled them together as two complementary and inseparable sets of priorities. School management, governors and
teachers slightly favoured the second of these two cards while parents and pupils
tended to favour the first. The first card suggests a more pupil-centred approach
while the second takes a more curriculum-centred approach. Students and staff
suggested that the balance of choice would have been tipped towards the first card
if it had, like the second, included the word 'all'. The inclusiveness of a curriculum
that met all needs was seen as the key feature of an effective school. We were also
reminded by teachers that it is merely rhetoric if the 'all' is not taken seriously and
imaginatively. It therefore had to be built from a genuine understanding of the
needs of pupils, and the curriculum on offer was often described as 'weak'. It failed

conspicuously to meet what students, or their teachers, perceived as skills that would help them survive in the world beyond the school gates.

Moral principles such as justice are promoted

- governors 0
- parents 9
- teachers 0
- pupils 30
- senior management 18

This card was not selected once by governors or teachers but was chosen by nearly one in three groups of students. It reflected students' concerns about fairness and equality of treatment, equality between the sexes and racial equality. Where it was not chosen by students, it was sometimes because the language of 'morality' had a stronger negative impact than the language of justice. This was also why some other groups of students rejected this card, wary of the 'high-flown' language of 'moral principles'. In the main it was not rejected as unimportant but excluded because it was not seen as one of the key indicators.

There are strong home–school links

- governors 20
- parents 50
- teachers 30
- pupils 5 and −10
- senior management 55

This card was most consistently selected by parents and senior management. It was six times more likely to be chosen by primary than secondary parents and three times as likely to be chosen by primary teachers. There was not the same differentiation between senior management and governors. It was one of the cards which most reflected different perspectives, priorities and understandings. For parents, it was their means of keeping in touch with their child's life in school. Senior management valued it both because it was high on the policy list and because, from their standpoint, good relationships promoted a much happier and effective school. For students, support from parents was seen as critical but parental links with school were not seen as particularly relevant to that. For some students, such links were to be positively discouraged because they undermined the student's own status and responsibility. Teachers were concerned about parents with whom they had no visible links and whose support for their children's learning might tip the balance between failure and success. It was much less likely to figure as a priority with secondary school teachers because linking mechanisms were seen as cumbersome and attempts to bring parents into school were seen as time consuming, often with little return.

Staff work collaboratively towards shared goals

- governors 20
- parents 25
- teachers 80
- pupils 15 and −10
- senior management 80

This card came at the top of the list for teachers and support staff because it was seen as an essential precondition of a successful school. It was also seen as an ambitious target and one to be strived for rather than one already attained. It could only be achieved, it was argued, in a school culture of talk, of willingness to co-operate and support one another, a culture in which problems were shared and there was a management team willing to listen. It was seen as impossible to achieve in an embattled school. Students often asked for an explanation of this card and were then more likely to see its value. Some of the less tractable young people were quick to see the downside of this and some argued that, in their experience, it put too much emphasis on staff–staff relationships and detracted from attention given to them. Secondary students quite often said that they did not recognise it as a feature of their school. It was a lower priority for parents and governors because the benefits were less apparent to them.

Collective worship takes place

- governors −55
- parents −55
- teachers −55
- pupils −55
- senior management −55

This was never placed in the top five but placed in the bottom three consistently by most groups. The case for rejection was often based on an adverse reaction to school assemblies or memories of ritualistic prayers and exhortation. In some schools, though, there were collective assemblies which were valued by staff, pupils and parents because they brought about greater insights into other cultures and faiths. The demotion of this card was usually on the basis of the word 'worship', which was seen as inappropriate for everyone in a school. The collective experience was frequently mentioned as important and to be valued.

7

WHAT HAPPENED NEXT?

What happened following the publication of 'Schools Speak for Themselves' is itself a fascinating case study of an idea whose time had come. It was seen by some as a risky move to publish 50,000 copies of the report and circulate them to all schools in England and Wales. Some within the NUT expected an adverse reaction from the membership but in fact none came, not a single phone call.

The launch of 'Schools Speak for Themselves' was held in the NUT headquarters in January 1996. The morning session was addressed by Her Majesty's Chief Inspector of Schools, Chris Woodhead, and the afternoon was given over to a presentation of the report. The event had been planned, and the agenda constructed, by the NUT leadership to present 'Schools Speak for Themselves' as a complement to external inspections and to open a constructive dialogue about the nature of external and internal evaluation. The report was extremely well received by the membership, although there was one comment from the floor to the effect that an OFSTED inspection sounded like a softer option than self-evaluation.

A positive and constructive meeting was held with Anthea Millett of the Teacher Training Agency (TTA) to consider how self-evaluation might permeate the thinking of teachers and impact on the teacher-as-researcher initiatives being promoted by the TTA. A follow-up meeting was also arranged with Chris Woodhead to explore the possibilities of closer collaboration. Discussions were civilised and robust but the Chief Inspector saw self-evaluation as something that had been tried and failed and the door was closed after us, politely but firmly.

We put the case for self-evaluation at both Labour Party and Conservative party conferences. Blackpool and Labour came first. Estelle Morris affirmed the Labour Party's commitment to self-evaluation and promised that it would be a part of government policy when New Labour came to power. It was a congenial and constructive occasion but left us unprepared for the reception that was to come at the Conservative Party conference the following week.

The presentation to the Conservatives in Bournemouth was altogether a more lively and combustible occasion. Eric Forth, the junior minister, apologised to his PPS for not delivering the carefully crafted speech prepared for him but he felt it was imperative to reply to 'the professor'. The case for self-evaluation, as presented, was, he said, antithetical to the main thrust of his government's policies: to lever up standards from the outside; to deal with 'rotten teachers and rotten schools'.

This message was warmly received by the bulk of his audience, some of whom responded with derision at the idea of 'self'-evaluation and in particular the involvement of pupils. As one delegate put it, 'The very thought that pupils could have anything useful to say is absurd. All they are interested in is the quality of the chips in the canteen.' The nature of interchange had also clearly convinced Doug McAvoy that constructive dialogue was no longer an option and he turned to the minister with a series of questions that exposed the differences between Conservative policies north and south of the border. Why, for example, were his colleagues in Scotland, including that most Thatcherite of Tories, Michael Forsyth, so persuaded by self-evaluation that they had put it at the heart of educational policy for the last half-decade?

It could never be said that the NUT had not tried hard to be pragmatic and conciliatory, arguing with a great deal more cool logic and evidence than the opposition. The case for self-evaluation continued to be presented at national and regional conferences over the next two years, including high-profile national conferences in September 1997 and November 1998 sponsored by the *Times Educational Supplement*, DEMOS and the NUT, with presentations from David Blunkett, Chris Woodhead, Anthea Millett, Michael Barber and Nick Tate.

Three training courses were held at Stoke Rochford and many of those who participated have written, sometimes at considerable length, to describe initiatives they took on return to their own schools or classrooms.

Between 1996 and 1997, the NUT sponsored a series of twelve articles on self-evaluation for the journal *Managing Schools Today*. These came from Australia, Canada, Denmark and Austria as well as from England and Scotland. They were written by academics, policy-makers and primary and secondary headteachers. They illustrated, with pull-out photocopiable protocols, a range of innovative and practical approaches to self-evaluation.

Putting self-evaluation on to the national agenda through constructive dialogue with OFSTED, the government and the opposition was the policy which the NUT continued to pursue. In July 1997 it published 'Evaluation, Inspection and Support: a system that works',[1] accepting the principle of school inspections but advocating a more integrated and negotiated approach, building on school self-evaluation and development planning. Copies of the NUT's recommendations were sent to the Government Task Force on Standards and distributed to its members in 1998.

At local authority level, self-evaluation or self-review was progressively being written into policy and 'Schools Speak for Themselves' was frequently used as a reference point for such policy formulation. Between 1996 and 1998, invitations came from close to 100 authorities to run workshops or address conferences on self-evaluation and school improvement. These were sometimes to introduce 'Schools Speak for Themselves', sometimes to give momentum to the authority's developing policy, or in some instances to help consolidate and review policies already in place. The most euphoric of these took place in Birmingham on 2 May 1997, with votes still coming in but a new Labour government assured. It was apt that this historic, educational milestone should have been celebrated in Birmingham. Its luminous commitment to self-evaluation and school improvement has come from the inside out, from a director of education ever prepared to exemplify through his own conduct and example how self-evaluation works.

The endorsement of self-evaluation by the government came, as had been promised by Estelle Morris, a few months later in the White Paper 'Excellence in

Schools'. Shortly after the general election Michael Barber was appointed to head the Standards and Effectiveness Unit of the DfEE, bringing with him a strong commitment to self-evaluation. He also brought in a team of advisers with an impressive portfolio of work in self-evaluation and school improvement – from the National Foundation for Educational Research, Cambridge's school improvement centre (Improving the Quality of Education for All: IQEA), Queensland's Quality Assurance Unit and from Sandringham School which was pursuing a bold and innovative approach to self-evaluation as part of the European Commission project.

In his book *The Learning Game* Michael Barber wrote: 'The essence of a successful organisation in this post-modern world is the search for improvement, and effective self-evaluation is the key to it.'[2] He describes self-evaluation as 'restless' in its quest for evidence, in a school's transparent sense of purpose, behaviour, relationships and classroom performance. He goes on to argue that internal and external evaluation are both essential and complementary in their relationship.

The publication by OFSTED in the spring of 1998 of its guide to self-evaluation was another important step forward in a national approach to evaluating schools.[3] The first five words of that document go right to the heart of self-evaluation; they are 'How good is our school?' These were the words that had provided the starting point for the NUT study and were the title of the Scottish Office policy document which has frequently been used in conjunction with 'Schools Speak for Themselves' in many English and Welsh authorities.[4]

The logic of posing that question implicitly acknowledges the value-judgement lying at the heart of the issue and suggests an open and exploratory approach to seeking the evidence. That is, after all, the motor and the fuel of school improvement. The signal weakness of the OFSTED document, however, was its failure to follow through on the logic of that question, to understand the crucial importance of the process or to address the central issues of concern to teachers and to learners. Its premise, that self-evaluation is based on an 'objective look' at pupils' achievements, leads it to concentrate almost exclusively on the statistics of assessment. This is not only a misuse of the term 'objective' but virtually ignores the subjective element, characteristic of the document itself and so crucial to an understanding of learning, teaching, ethos and organisational development.

The dichotomy between 'objective' and 'subjective' in school evaluation is, in fact, a misleading distraction. There is an interesting analogy with temperature, the objective measure of which is the height mercury rises in the glass at a given place, time and height off the ground. As a rough proxy for how you are going to feel, it is undoubtedly useful, but the American invention of the wind-chill index and more recently the heat index indicate how you really feel, which may be fifteen to twenty degrees different from the temperature. Furthermore, if you are a small person on a hot pavement on a busy New York street, you will feel different from a tall person walking across the grass of Central Park. Nor is heat simply some external force which acts on people as passive recipients. People also generate heat and warm up cold rooms, yet, misled by a belief in objectivity, they continue to hold futile arguments about whether the room is 'too hot' or 'too cold' when both statements are simultaneously true in terms of individual experience.

Hopefully, over time, we will come to a more sophisticated understanding of measurement and *Evaluation Matters* will be revisited with a broader vision. This is likely to happen as greater exposure is given to the excellent self-evaluation practice going on in many schools, focused on learning and concerned to address in a rigorous and comprehensive way the central question: 'How good is *our* school?'

SCHOOLS AND AUTHORITIES SPEAKING
FOR THEMSELVES

Two years on from the launch of the publication the NUT were interested in more systematic evidence of the impact of 'Schools Speak for Themselves'. How had it been received by authorities and schools? Was it being used by advisory services, by schools, by classroom teachers? And if so, how?

Independent consultants were engaged to collect data, to visit schools and authorities and conduct interviews. To get anything like a comprehensive national picture would have required an ingenious, ambitious and costly research design. As it was, the researchers wrote to every authority in England and Wales, asking for information on their use or knowledge of 'Schools Speak for Themselves'. We knew from previous studies that cold-call letters rarely find their way back to their authors and that speculative telephone calls lead into a tortuous series of referrals. And this was the nature of the experience in the follow-up project.

Organisations tend to know less than their members, and this was often revealed in accounts of what was, or was not, happening in an authority or school. Accounts were generally given with complete conviction and integrity but often in the absence of any shared knowledge of ongoing developments at classroom, school or authority level.

We also knew from previous studies that documents sent to headteachers rarely find their way to classrooms. Trickle down does not work; trickle up does not necessarily work either. The route of a document into a school via a teacher, as was the case with many of the NUT documents, does not guarantee that it will ever find its way to the headteacher or senior management team. The serendipitous nature of the way documents come to light is revealed in this comment from one local authority adviser: 'My awareness of "Schools Speak for Themselves" only came into being through a visit to a school which had received a copy via the NUT.'

It was not uncommon to find schools using 'Schools Speak for Themselves' without the authority being aware of the existence of the document. There were also authorities where 'Schools Speak for Themselves' had framed policy but teachers and headteachers knew little about it. There were schools where headteachers were wedded to a 'Schools Speak for Themselves' approach while individual teachers were unaware of it, and there were cases of individual teachers using the document in their own classrooms unknown to the headteacher – occasionally quite studiedly.

We learned a lot about how authorities work, who speaks to whom and how knowledge is passed on, or not passed on. Restructuring of inspection and advisory services meant that people arrived in new and unfamiliar jobs while others left, taking with them expertise and networks built up over a lifetime. The move to unitary authorities was another complicating factor in eroding collective memory. The following comments were not untypical:

Unfortunately we are a new small authority, one of five smaller units of the old authority. In these circumstances, and with the complete restructuring of directorate and advisory services, it is extremely difficult to locate answers to your questions or the documentation to which you refer. Nor can we at this stage easily gather information on what individual schools are actually doing.

Although our inquiries revealed communication lacunae and bureaucratic blocks, there emerged a picture not so much of inefficiency or busywork that critics like to portray, but of people under pressure, unable to meet the multiple demands on them, often isolated from their colleagues by those pressures and apologetic about their lack of knowledge. There were many examples of goodwill and good intentions; for example, 'Organised follow-up [to "Schools Speak for Themselves"] was intended but the pressure on a very small inspectorate team having to respond to externally imposed imperatives let plans slip off the agenda.' One headteacher who wrote positively about the document nonetheless concluded apologetically, 'I didn't have the heart to ask for detailed examination of yet another detailed document system on top of everything else.'

All of this could have provided a fascinating study of the organisation of educational services in millennial Britain but the primary purpose was to find examples of authorities, schools and individuals who had picked up ideas and developed practice from 'Schools Speak for Themselves', and to ascertain to what extent it had been criticised, rejected or put aside in favour of something more relevant and useful.

We asked authorities to refer us on to schools that had been using 'Schools Speak for Themselves'. We also sent letters to schools and authorities who had held courses or had ordered the publication. This was to prove a more fruitful approach. While it necessarily adds bias to our sample, we should not presuppose that because a school or authority requested the document, or had sent staff on a training course, that this would necessarily lead to positive evaluation or practical use. Nor does it invalidate the accounts from authorities, schools and individuals who reported positively, and sometimes evangelically, about the impact and usefulness of the 'Schools Speak for Themselves' approach.

What follows, then, is a summary of the written responses from forty-one authorities and fifty-five schools who provided us with information. Visits and interviews in eight schools and eight authorities gave us an opportunity to explore issues in more depth. The following analysis aims to be as balanced an account as possible, allowing schools and authorities to speak for themselves without any editorialising on the part of the author.

THE AUTHORITIES

The analysis of written replies from authorities revealed a range of contexts and uses of 'Schools Speak for Themselves'. These included:

- authority-wide conferences

- workshops for senior and/or middle management
- school-based INSET
- governors' meetings
- governor training
- information/training for advisory staff

Some authorities also made specific references, such as meetings/workshops for:

- clusters of primary headteachers
- the Joint Advisory Committee of the Education Committee
- Trade Union Standing Committee

Authorities described a range of different purposes served by 'Schools Speak for Themselves'. These were:

- to raise the awareness of advisers and to inform their practice
- to inform local authority inspectorate
- to provide tools for school use
- to support schools in setting up their own self-evaluation
- to exemplify good practice
- helping in the review of leadership and management
- raising standards of attainment in teaching and learning
- in preparation for, or follow up to, OFSTED inspections

The variety of purposes and contexts of its use are illustrated in this comment from Wiltshire Local Authority:

> 'Schools Speak for Themselves' has been used in courses/conferences with primary, secondary and special school heads to show good practice/value for money approaches to school self-review/evaluation. Used in specific schools in twilight seminars with secondary middle managers to illustrate self-review tools for use in monitoring the work of a department or year group.

Other uses, purposes and benefits were also described by authorities. These included statements such as, it is 'helpful in persuading schools to collect evidence', 'it is a key to the development of a self-evaluation culture', 'linking it with school improvement planning, literacy audits, action plans, early years development plans, behaviour management'. One adviser wrote, 'I incorporated some of the ideas into a course on "Information Governors Need" and another on "Marketing the School".'

Some authorities commented specifically on its relevance for classroom teachers. For example, 'I am particularly interested in improving teachers' "belief" in their children' and 'It illuminated the next step in teacher involvement in quality assurance once the current vogue of vindictiveness is over.'

It was used by some authorities to link with appraisal systems and to tie appraisal and whole-school evaluation into a more coherent approach. Three authorities described the linking of authority inspections with headteacher in-service. For example, in Nottinghamshire, 'Schools Speak for Themselves' was used to inform an innovative approach to appraisal in which outside consultants worked with headteachers, gathering data from multiple sources and using them to set both professional and school development targets.

There were numerous comments on the importance of 'Schools Speak for Them-selves' as a complement or 'counterbalance' to the OFSTED framework. One example from a registered inspector:

> It has helped me in my work as an OFSTED inspector . . . It enabled me to put self-reflection into the work I do . . . It also made me realise that a rigid, inflexible system of OFSTED inspections, which did not involve schools in self-evaluation, and the subsequent development planning based on it, is a waste of time and money.

Most authorities already had review systems in place or were in the process of developing or redeveloping their approach. One authority wrote, 'Sorry not to be more helpful. We have our own in-house school review system.' The typical response, however, was for authorities to say that they had drawn on 'Schools Speak for Themselves' along with other sources to inform and shape their own approach to review; for example, as a reference for the LEA in setting up its own system or as 'a cornerstone of LEA policy'. The following are examples from two authorities:

> Kent LEA has a major scheme of supported school self-review. Since its inception our scheme documentation carries reference to and recom-mendation for 'Schools Speak for Themselves'. Some 300 plus schools have now joined the scheme. We found it *very* helpful in establishing the underpinning principles and framework of the Kent approach.

> We have publicised and used 'Schools Speak for Themselves' throughout the courses we provide locally for our Leadership Programme. This included provision at all leadership levels from administrator to headteacher. I have also recommended it to Governing Bodies to aid their development. The unfortunate omission of leadership and management is a weakness in our view as we have used other sources and our own thinking to rectify this.[5]

Some authorities had formally evaluated the pack, in some cases against other available material:

> 'A small group of headteachers, deputies and teachers evaluated 'Schools Speak for Themselves' against other currently available models in terms of usefulness and relevance. They considered it offered a practical, workable resource bank for schools to use to develop their own practice. [It] came out as favourite.

I evaluated 8 packs last year and SSFT was the joint leader (with Kirklees' pack).

I conducted a review of the literature of school review and found that the SSFT approach was one that we strongly recommended to headteachers.

Extremely relevant – particularly the Teaching and Learning sections. We will be using it a great deal more in the coming year as we look at Teaching and Learning in our School Improvement sessions with headteachers.

Specific comments were made about the following:

- clear layout and structure
- useful and practical
- examples of good practice
- classroom based
- friendly
- can be used in a wide range of contexts
- helps systematic collection of evidence
- NUT sponsorship enhanced credibility

There were a few comments on the relevance of the document under a new government seeking to support teachers and put education into the forefront of policy. One authority described 'Schools Speak for Themselves' as 'linking clearly with the main themes of government policy'. Another wrote: 'There can never have been a more important time for the approaches outlined in the document to be supported, listened to, encouraged.'

There were also comments on the difficulties and obstacles to using the 'Schools Speak for Themselves' approach more fully. One authority adviser wrote: 'We have difficulty in seeing where this fits into our current cycle of development planning.' Another: 'The domination of the OFSTED criteria makes it difficult for schools to accommodate another set of criteria for self-evaluation.' A number described the momentum being lost as other priorities overtook the authority's planning. Where there were such difficulties, these were frequently also accompanied by requests for advice and suggestions as to future development work. 'We would welcome advice and support on taking it forward' was a typical comment. In fact a number of authorities – Cheshire, Hillingdon, Stockport, Newcastle – are in the process of conducting, or setting up, pilot studies. A fuller account of Newcastle's experience is given at the end of this chapter.

IMPACT AT SCHOOL LEVEL

Written comments from individual schools were of two main kinds. One referred to the 'Schools Speak for Themselves' approach as a management tool or lever for change at whole-school level. The second set of comments referred to very specific uses by individual teachers or departments. SSFT was described as 'a powerful tool in the management of change'. A Walsall head wrote: 'Our whole-school effectiveness process is based on models suggested in "Schools Speak for Themselves".' A Wolverhampton head wrote: 'It has confirmed my view that a school-led, LEA-supported, quality assurance model is the way for schools to get to grips with monitoring/review/evaluation', and from a Sunbury head: 'Opinions were sought and highlighted through staff, pupils and governors. I used it as a strategy to encourage (demand!) greater involvement in the school by the governors and to encourage student input into school improvement.' A chair of governors wrote:

> We have conducted surveys of pupils' attitudes to school, and we have extended our assessment of pupils to include detailed analysis of such areas as concentration, personal organisation, relationships and contribution to school life, all measured against specific indicators across the primary age range. This information is shared with parents as an attempt to maintain and share our view that there is more to life than Level 4.

St Julian's School, Quinta Nova, Portugal wrote:

> It has helped enormously with the work we have been undertaking to receive ECIS accreditation. This process is closely allied to their self-evaluating school concept. Questionnaires were used with staff, students, parents and the community to aid us with self-evaluation and development planning. Some difficult and challenging questions have arisen, including the desirability of an on-going Parents' Association or an alternative home–school contract.

Other comments referred to a range of specific purposes, uses and benefits:

- monitoring and improving approaches to numeracy and literacy
- evaluation of homework
- evaluation of discipline and behaviour policies
- as a basis for INSET
- awareness-raising seminars for governors
- involving parents more in evaluating and contributing to development planning
- monitoring learning and teaching
- peer classroom observation
- developing roles of staff (e.g. RE co-ordinator, learning support co-ordinator)
- involving governors in systematic evaluation of the school
- helping to develop a more corporate ethos in the school

The importance focusing on the classroom is emphasised in the following comment from the headteacher of the Beacon School in Surrey:

> Independent learning, a sense of purpose accompanied by pace, high expectations, challenging work, targeting and reviewing progress, relevant and focused records of achievement; all these are key aspects of effectiveness; schools should also challenge staff who label pupils, or who blame

them for their own failings. The social development of the individual is also of vital importance. All this is mainly common sense, but it is refreshing to hear it agreed upon by educationalists. The main feature of Strathclyde's research is that it all evolves from teachers themselves.

CLASSROOM LEVEL

The biggest challenge to quality assurance and school improvement is their accessibility to, and use by, classroom teachers. We received replies from thirty-four classroom teachers who had attended courses on 'Schools Speak for Themselves' and/or used the document in practical ways in their own classrooms. All replies were positive, some others reinforcing existing beliefs, consolidating or changing thinking and attitudes. The majority (twenty-six of the thirty-four) had put ideas to positive use; for example:

- helping to relate the school development plan more closely to classroom teaching
- evaluating classroom practice against key criteria
- involving pupils in evaluating and improving teaching
- setting targets
- involving parents in evaluating learning

The enthusiasm of some teachers had been dampened by lack of endorsement from their heads. Some had, in spite of that, put the ideas into practice within their own classrooms. One teacher commented, 'As a class teacher I have been unable to use the strategies in the school. I tried to discuss the framework with the head but he was not receptive and has since left. But self-evaluation is ongoing in an informal way in my own classroom.'

Others said they had found it difficult to advocate with other evaluation strategies already in place:

> Our current self-evaluation systems continue to operate as part of a bureaucratic-imposed model of management. Much of the paperwork is completed in a ritualistic manner and there is some evidence of documents being changed by members of the senior management team in order to avoid discussion of staff perceptions that are unflattering. My belief is that our organisation lacks the confidence to put into practice much of the 'Schools Speak for Themselves' philosophy.

Many teachers commented on the strengths of self-evaluation in comparison to the OFSTED framework, but these statements were almost always accompanied by positive and forward-looking proposals. Irrespective of whether ideas had as yet been translated into practice, there were many plans for the future.

> The high levels of focused debate provoked by the self-evaluation will, I believe, be invaluable in giving further direction to the development of

Boreham Primary School in a way that will give ownership to the process of improvement to all members of the school community.

The change in my attitudes has been immense but old habits die hard. I am getting better at working with the new cultural ethos – the spirit is willing.

USING THE OFSTED CARD SORT

We were sent three detailed case studies from schools that had used the OFSTED card sort as a way of stimulating dialogue and establishing priorities.

Stoke Primary School in Coventry used the OFSTED card sort in the first instance with staff. Working in four small groups, the nineteen staff agreed a top five which included, from all four groups, 'staff work co-operatively towards shared goals' and 'there are high expectations of all pupils'.

The same exercise was then undertaken with parents, governors and staff together, comparing results with the guiding principles of the school which had been agreed seven years previously in 1990. The benefit of this exercise was in revisiting and refining those principles and turning them into concrete indicators which the school could use to evaluate itself against. The priority given in the card sort to home–school links by governors as well as parents provided the basis for a questionnaire later sent out to parents. The 120 responses which came back led to the identification of specific areas of priority to be addressed by the school.

A similar approach to Stoke's was adopted in Holly Bank School in West York-shire. It is a school which accommodates students with profound and multiple learning difficulties. The OFSTED card sort, with words adapted to fit the school's own context, produced five agreed priorities:

- shared teamwork
- everyone's views are listened to and they feel their contributions are valued
- deployment of resources is the result of a shared, negotiated approach
- there are places for students/tenants to go and constructive things to do at all times
- students/tenants have forums for discussing their concerns and problems

Staff were then asked to find ways of measuring each of these five priorities. A questionnaire was designed on the two-axis-model – school now and the ideal school. Staff were asked to respond to the seventy items, giving their views on how they saw the school currently and what they saw as important goals for the future. Responses were then fed back at an in-service staff development day and used to shape priorities for the future.

USING THE INDICATORS

Groby Community College in Leicestershire used the indicators suggested in 'Schools Speak for Themselves' to review their own practice. Developments linked to these indicators included:

- rewriting goals and codes of student behaviour with training days to support staff in implementing these
- a broad range student achievements being celebrated with photographs around the school
- increasing student motivation through the introduction of reward systems
- good-quality data on attainment and targets for parents
- review of communication systems within the school and between home and school
- inclusion of support staff in all aspects of the school's development
- making reception areas more inviting and accessible to parents
- questionnaires and consultation with parents on a range of issues
- closer collaboration with neighbouring high schools, 'talking up' each other's qualities
- establishment of a working party to monitor security arrangements.

Another example of using the indicators comes from East Sussex Authority where an in-service day for headteachers was used to consider how specific indicators could be addressed at the levels of the local education authority, the school and the classroom teacher. Heads worked in ten groups, each with one of the indicator clusters, making recommendations to the authority. So, for example, in relation to the indicator set 'Support for Learning', these were the key points, recommendations and issues raised by each group:

Local education authority

- technology for processing information and feedback
- guidelines on homework

School

- celebrating success in and out of school: pupils and staff
- evaluation of use of library to encourage independent learning
- audit of learning styles, experience, attainment

Teacher

- having clear objectives about learning and sharing them with pupils
- how to challenge appropriately
- involvement of pupils in self-evaluation

THE INTERNATIONAL CONTEXT

The impact of 'Schools Speak for Themselves' was not simply at a national level. How ideas travel across national boundaries is a fruitful topic for further research, but, by whatever route, 'Schools Speak for Themselves' managed to find its way into distant lands. In the two years since its publication it has been translated (in part or whole) into Italian, Danish and Thai, and places in which conferences, presentations or extended workshops have been held include the following:

- Italy – Bergamo, Trento, Pisa
- Germany – Gütersloh, Lippestadt
- Denmark – Copenhagen, Billund, Odense, Middelfahrt
- Netherlands – Twente
- Iceland – Akureyri, Reykjavik
- Thailand – Bangkok
- Singapore
- Australia – Brisbane, Sydney, Cairns
- United States – Chicago
- Canada – Montreal, Quebec
- Argentina – Buenos Aires
- Uzbekistan – Tashkent
- Hong Kong

Among the vehicles for this dissemination have been national and international conferences. The NUT study was presented at the BERA, SERA, ECER and AERA (the British, Scottish, European and American Research Association conferences, respectively) and at the International Congress on School Effectiveness and School Improvement in Memphis, Tennessee.

In Pisa in April 1998 a conference was held bringing together the European Committee for Education, the European Parents' Association, the European Secondary Heads Association and OBESSU (the European Union of School Students) – the last was the prime mover in organising the conference. The theme was Quality in Education and self-evaluation was centre stage. Day one of the conference was given over to a rerun of the 'Schools Speak for Themselves' process with mixed groups of students, teachers, parents and heads. A video of the conference captures the dialogue that took place, and an extract from the *Times Educational Supplement* describes one of those moments of truth when the dynamic and dialogic nature of self-evaluation was crystallised.

The NUT study was also a backdrop to a high-profile development of the European Commission's 'Evaluating Quality in School Education', involving 101 schools in eighteen countries. In all of these the common centrepiece was an evaluation of the school by students, teachers, parents and governors (or school boards). Many of the schools involved, despite initial reservations, have ventured further than they thought possible, exceeding their own expectations.

Chapter 8 examines approaches to evaluation in very different country contexts with different administrative and political constraints. It illustrates that self-evaluation has become a major international movement and that 'Schools Speak for Themselves' was very much a child of its time.

TWO CASE STUDIES

1 Asmall Primary School

Anne Waterhouse

> Asmall Primary School has many good, and some unusual fea-
> tures. It is a developing school, continually seeking to improve its
> performance. The staff and governors are aware of the school's
> strengths, and areas in need of further development.[6]

This opening paragraph of the OFSTED report of the first inspection of the school
in November 1997 gives a very clear reflection of a school with a long tradition of
self-evaluation as a strategy for school improvement. The inspection took place
during my last few weeks as the headteacher of the school. This short case study is
written from my personal perspective and is an ideal opportunity for me to reflect
upon my period of headship and the professional development benefits for myself
and my colleagues deriving from our involvement with 'Schools Speak for
Themselves'.

I was attracted to the project because it sought to go beyond the OFSTED framework for inspection to open up new possibilities and alternative approaches. I saw
it as enabling us to get a firmer grip on our accountability as well as helping us to
identify realistic and achievable improvement strategies. It was also an opportunity to consider the role of the critical friend in school improvement.

As a primary head, I had always believed that school improvement should be
closely related to what teachers do and think within the wider context of developments at school, district and national levels. As a new headteacher in 1984, I
believed that I needed to work with my new colleagues to identify the areas for
improvement rather than coming in and imposing my own views.

To this end, I used a range of self-evaluation approaches, continuously updating
and customising them, trying to find the approach which would enhance our confidence as a staff and our ability to evaluate ourselves. Initially I used one of the
early models for school self-review, *Guidelines for Review and Internal Development*
(GRIDS) and later an amended version of the *Diagnosis of Individual and Organisational Needs* (DION). I also used the twelve factors that were identified as being
within the control of the head and teachers, sharing these with the governing
body who were becoming progressively comfortable with the process of school
self-review.

We used the LEA's own approach to self-evaluation and, as this was overtaken
by the introduction of OFSTED, we put to use both original and new versions of
the OFSTED framework to review the work of the school, helping us to identify
our strengths and weaknesses. I believed that we also needed the external perspective and saw it as important that as a staff we became more confident with outsiders' assessment of us. I therefore took up every possible opportunity to invite
other people into the school to work with the staff. So, when we were invited to

participate in the 'Schools Speak for Themselves' project, it presented an ideal opportunity to widen our experience with external critical friends.

In July 1995 two researchers from the Quality in Education Centre at the University of Strathclyde visited the school. As well as collecting data to inform the research, the project modelled a process for data collection.

Two key questions were asked of different groups within the school community:

- What, in your view, are the key characteristics of a 'good' school?
- Given a set of 23 criteria, derived from OFSTED, which of these do you rate as most important and least important for your school?

As headteacher, I found this stage of the process very threatening. It was what was known in the school as 'a sticky armpit' situation. I felt extremely anxious about how I should respond if the exercise revealed wide disparities in views among the different members of the school community. Looking back I suppose that was because we had been driving the self-evaluation work ourselves and I had avoided areas which might be contentious and split relationships. However, to my relief and pride, support staff and administrative staff, teaching staff, governors and parents, and the children in their own way, all responded similarly in identifying the same range of criteria. The realisation that parents and governors shared the same values as the school staff was hugely gratifying. That we now had evidence to show we were all working together towards common goals was a particularly powerful moment.

With this solid grounding in shared values, the final part of the research was to discuss how we might go about gathering evidence as to our performance on the agreed criteria. To this end we used the framework suggested in 'Schools Speak for Themselves'. The following is an example of issues identified in one individual cluster: 'Support for Learning'.

Indicator: 'Pupils see themselves as independent learners'

Quantitative evidence

- use/take-up of learning support
- number of pupils receiving help
- pupils use of self-study time
- use of library
- use of software
- use of resource materials
- balance of teaching/independent learning time

Qualitative evidence

- pupils' views of themselves as learners
- views of learning support by staff, pupils, parents and governors
- atmosphere in classrooms
- attitudes of pupils

Methods/instruments

- analysis of learning support use by category/status of pupil
- interviews with pupils of varying abilities
- logs of pupil use of time
- assessment of learning styles

The whole process from identification of criteria to tools for evaluation itself was regarded as valuable by participants. Almost without exception, respondents claimed to be pleased to have been involved in the process and happy to have been invited to contribute their views.

It did not stop there, however. Improvement is a continuous process and one of the crucial elements for me was the involvement of a critical friend. Without this, I would not have had the confidence to move the school forward into the next phase of self-evaluation, one involving external evaluation against predetermined criteria.

Following 'Schools Speak for Themselves', I suggested that the school should seek recognition as an Investor in People (IIP) so that public recognition could be given to the quality of the staff's work and to help us prepare further for the arrival of OFSTED inspectors. IIP is promoted by the Department for Education and Employment as part of its Improving Schools initiative and demonstrates a systematic approach to school self-improvement through the use of a five-stage cycle. In August 1996 the school became the first in the area to achieve IIP recognition.

Although we had made dramatic improvements in terms of whole-school development and coherent school development planning, I was still not content that we had made enough impact on what was happening in individual classrooms. This meant making the school development plan more focused on teaching and learning and including percentage targets for pupils' achievements against end of Key Stage criteria. The OFSTED inspection in November 1997 confirmed what we had come to recognise – the need to address, as a matter of urgency, inconsistencies in the quality of teaching.

While the OFSTED inspection recognised contributions that had been made over the years by self-evaluating strategies and acknowledged 'examples of outstanding and exemplary practice', it endorsed our own growing belief that we needed to move on from whole-school initiatives into individual classrooms and into the hearts and minds of all staff.

The inspection process was, however, viewed in a negative light by the staff. It undermined the confidence of experienced and highly effective teachers and, from a personal point of view, was one of the most negative periods of my professional life as a teacher.

My involvement in 'Schools Speak for Themselves', on the other hand, was one of the most powerful professional development experiences of my career to date. Not only did the report provide me, as a headteacher, with qualitative and quantitative strategies for analysing and planning school improvement, it also provided me with a resource bank of materials in my new role as an LEA adviser. My experiences in schools, culminating with feeling a total victim of the OFSTED process in comparison with the positive nature of school self-evaluation, have convinced me that my early convictions about ownership and involvement were right. However, I do believe that the role of a critical friend is crucial. Unlike the current OFSTED hit-and-run model, external accountability and school improvement need to work hand in hand with schools being offered support to ensure that effective teaching and learning improves the quality of classroom experiences for every child.

2 Newcastle Local Authority

Roger Edwardson, Assistant Director of Education

Historically, Newcastle has provided a ready jobs market for a low-skilled work-force in heavy industry. High levels of educational achievement have not been required to earn a living. Consequently, aspirations towards educational goals have been difficult to promote. Levels of attainment for eleven-year-olds and sixteen-year-olds are unacceptably low. Corporately, the City Council wishes to address these issues, emphasising the importance of formal qualifications and skills for employment, as well as supporting individuals in developing their capacity to take a full and active part in the life of the city.

Newcastle LEA embarked on its school improvement strategy early in the summer of 1996. It was clear that a new approach to school development planning was necessary if schools were to target underachievement. The Advisory Service set about identifying the factors which inhibit children's progress and emphasising the need to improve teaching quality and raise expectations of what the city's children could and should achieve. The strategy recognised that raising standards was complex and often a slow process. It recognised that there is no single approach by which schools can maximise the potential of all pupils. However, it did endorse target-setting within a clear framework of development as one way in which pupils could be helped to improve their performance.

The strategy recognised that school improvement was most likely to be effective when the process is owned by the school and the staff, not imposed from outside. Yet, it is also clear that there is no such thing as a self-sufficient school. Drawing on the resources of the community and the LEA is vital to school improvement, not just to raise standards of achievement but also to strengthen the linkage between the classroom and its urban context. Targeting the support of a range of agencies, including social services and the health authority, generates closer collaboration, and makes more effective use of resources to raise achievement in schools. Working with local communities engages parents more effectively in their children's learning by improving their own capacity to learn. There is also a challenge in the uncertainty about which features actually make a difference in school improvement. There is little doubt that effective leadership by the headteacher is a key element but defining the paramount elements of effective leadership is more problematic. What is clear is that the effective headteacher develops a shared sense of purpose and promotes concerted action to work towards a limited number of key objectives. The most effective change agents are those who have learning and teaching as the touchstones of their approach.

Good schools are staffed with good teachers and it is the teaching force that delivers the motivation and encouragement for pupils to improve their standards.

There is no simple recipe for school improvement, especially for the most hard-pressed schools, but it is clear, and in Newcastle this has been demonstrated, that schools do make a difference. Schools which evaluate themselves regularly make an even greater difference.

Soon after my appointment in 1996, the National Union of Teachers published an excellent document, which was to become a major school improvement tool in the city – 'Schools Speak for Themselves'. The NUT publication was timely. As part of a strategy which asked schools to revisit their school development plan and to involve all teachers in the process, I invited Professor John MacBeath from the Quality in Education Centre (QIE) at the University of Strathclyde and John Bangs from the NUT to launch their publication in the city. The conference was very well attended – the fact that more than 70 per cent of Newcastle teachers are NUT members was a significant help. 'Schools Speak for Themselves' is utilised in all Newcastle schools, and they have actively used a range of the tools within the document, often on training days, with governors and with pupils themselves. This was a very powerful approach to a policy to support school self-evaluation. Quoting from the NUT document:

> If we are able to pool that collective wisdom, it would enable us to con-struct a widely shared, or even national, framework for school self-evaluation. Such a framework could suggest a range of ways of going about the process and it might identify those which appear promising and most cost-effective. It would also allow a more considered judgement on the place and purpose of external evaluation and its relationship to internal school evaluation.

Following a further publication, by the Scottish Office, 'How Good Is Our School?', schools in Newcastle were provided with further support for self-evaluation. The performance indicators identified in this document proved very useful as a basis for an audit of effectiveness. This approach was also used as a pilot in twelve schools as part of a collaborative review involving the advisory service and the management team in the schools.

It is clear from our experience that there is a need to examine the strengths and weaknesses of external and internal evaluation and the relevance of criteria and data. The real issue must always be how the information gained from both pro-cesses can be used to support teachers' priorities for evaluation which will inevitably and rightly be the effectiveness of the teaching and learning.

School self-evaluation is a major focus of our improvement strategy. Good teachers using the most effective methods are clearly the key to higher standards. We need to invest in our teaching force, to raise their self-esteem and build on the skills and knowledge they have developed so successfully over many years. The government's White Paper, 'Excellence in Schools', is a first-class document and deserves to be read and reread. Clearly investment in education is much needed after eighteen years in which schools and local authorities have been heavily criti-cised for low standards while not possessing the resources to address the issues. Not only do we need to invest in our teaching force, we also need to work more closely with universities and researchers to identify and disseminate the evident good practice in classrooms. As the White Paper states, 'All the evidence indicates that standards rise fastest where schools themselves take responsibility for their own improvement.'

Most schools clearly need and welcome assistance and support to raise standards, and local authorities are working harder than ever to help. Newcastle's inspection and advisory service is no exception and has, for example, withdrawn from contracting for OFSTED inspections. It is developing a new framework for school reviews which will actively involve the management team of the school directly in lesson observation. More importantly, the monitoring, which takes the form of day visits, subject and school reviews, will be more clearly linked to the school's own improvement targets and will report on the progress made in achieving its targets.

Reviews are most effective when they provide quality feedback to teachers about the strengths and weaknesses of the teaching and learning. Because of the presence of OFSTED, unlike in the Scottish system, there has been a predominant focus on teaching quality rather than learning. The consequence of this is that external evaluation has not always been as successful as it might have been in raising standards. In some cases – for example, when a school has been placed in special measures – pupil performance significantly falls.

Effective school management has always been crucial in raising standards. This is particularly so when managers are actively involved in evaluation and the development of teachers in the classroom. Such evaluation should be extended to involve the middle managers, the heads of departments in secondary schools and the subject co-ordinators in primary schools. More usually, senior managers are actively observing lessons and feeding back to teachers their strengths and weaknesses, although there is no evidence that this continues during the actual inspection week. When this is done well the culture also seems to have an impact on pupils themselves. They seem more aware of their own achievements and are actively involved in monitoring their own learning. In good schools this information is available, usually through some form of pupil profile, to parents, and so the circle is complete. These schools might be described as learning organisations; a phrase often used by a very senior DfEE official as being one of the goals they wish to achieve.

I do believe we are now closer to pooling the collective wisdom on school evaluation to the point where we can construct a widely shared, national framework for schools' self-evaluation. In this process local authorities have a crucial role to play. The resulting framework should incorporate the best approaches from north and south of the border. Newcastle is well placed, at least geographically, as it benefits from both. It would, as John MacBeath so rightly suggests in the NUT publication, 'allow a more considered judgement of the place and purpose of external evaluation and its relationship to internal school evaluation'. I look forward to further developments which I am sure this government will wish to pursue.

8

WHAT HAPPENS IN OTHER COUNTRIES?

There was a time when schools were schools and teachers were left alone to get on with the business of teaching. It is now universally recognised that such a system cannot guarantee that children will be allowed to get on with the business of learning and that a healthy educational system is open and inviting of improvement and accountability.

In Denmark it is a tradition of long standing that teachers close their classroom doors and headteachers respect their professional autonomy. Together with small classes, excellent conditions of service and no local or national inspectorate, it is not surprising that many Danish teachers are resisting reforms that will require them to be more accountable for what happens in their classrooms. External evaluation is on its way in Denmark and in response many schools, authorities and teachers' unions are looking to self-evaluation as the bridge between the old and the new.

Denmark is not alone in this. Other countries are searching for a system that will bring a stronger sense of accountability but at the same time respect the professionalism of teachers and the integrity of the school as a self-evaluating organisation. Some countries, with self-evaluation already established, are looking to find the best approach to external review. Others, with external systems of review already in place, have stepped back from the traditional inspectorial approach.

The Norwegian educator Trond Alvik describes three different forms that internal/external evaluation can take.[1] These are:

- Parallel. That is both school and external review body conduct their own evaluations. They may afterwards share and compare findings.
- Sequential. The school conducts its own evaluation and then the external body uses that as a basis for its review. This may work in the opposite direction. The external body furnishes the school with feedback or findings which they then work on.
- Co-operative. The two parties discuss and negotiate the process and different interests and viewpoints are taken into account simultaneously.

These are useful categories for describing how different countries are trying to accommodate the evaluation of schools to the unique context and history of their own systems.

EUROPE

Only a few European countries have a national inspectorate and where these exist their role is under review. Austria, for example, has had an inspectorate for many years but their relationship to schools is currently in the process of change to become less a monitoring body and more a resource for schools. Their role will be to support schools in the process of self-evaluation, working alongside them to develop the tools for self-improvement. Some of the most imaginative, leading-edge work in self-evaluation can be found in Austria, where researchers at the University of Innsbruck are working closely with the Ministry of Education in helping to shape what Alvik would describe as a 'co-operative' approach.

Something similar is happening in the Netherlands. As in Austria, there is close collaboration between researchers and policy-makers in developing new models. The University of Twente has, for more than a decade, conducted pioneering work in school effectiveness and is now using that knowledge base to help put in place a 'sequential' system in which the school conducts its own evaluation first, with the role of external inspection being to validate the quality of the school's own internal processes. The Netherlands is, like many other countries, highly decentralised and their chief inspector actively encourages variety in approaches, so schools have at their disposal many sources of readily available good advice. For example, a publi-cation from the national association for school students, *Checklist om een Gouden School to Worden*, provides guidelines for students on how to evaluate learning and teaching, organisation, communication and relationships, describing what part students should play in helping to improve all of these.[2]

Italy is another example of a decentralised system where in certain provinces self-evaluation has been given a high profile. Although there has been a body of inspectors for many years, they have never systematically evaluated schools. With an Act of 1997, however, the inspectorate will be given a national role through the setting up of a new agency called Service for Quality in Education. It will provide technical support for schools and define criteria which schools can use for their own self-evaluation.

Spain has no external inspection but the Spanish Ministry of Education has in the last few years been moving progressively towards a sequential model of self-evaluation whose purpose is to 'bring about an in-depth renewal of the learning process'. In 1997 the Ministry published an attractive set of six volumes on how to go about 'autoevaluación', each volume presenting different stages and facets of the process – purposes, resources needed, questionnaires, case studies, procedures for analysis and interpretation.[3] In their scheme teacher and 'client' satisfaction count for nearly one-third of the total rating for school quality.

In countries where inspectors have traditionally evaluated individual teachers but not schools – Germany, France and Belgium, for example – there has also been a recent reappraisal of their role and an increasing emphasis on finding a school-based approach to self-evaluation. In Germany, where reform is taking place at state rather than national level, the role of the inspectorate in Bremen is to become, 'an agency for support and consultancy'. Wessen and North-Rhein Westphalia see it in similar terms. The Bertelsmann Foundation has given a powerful impetus to self-evaluation through close collaboration with state administrations and with the

Office of the Presidency, bringing together consultants from other countries with successful self-evaluation in place. They also support national and international projects and awards to innovative schools and progressive practice. In 1996 the Foundation awarded a prize for schools and authorities with innovative approaches to self-evaluation and in 1997 initiated a seven-country project to develop and network good practice in school self-evaluation.[4]

In the last few years the European Commission has sponsored a number of self-evaluation projects under their Socrates Programme. One of these, 'Evaluating Quality in School Education', has documented examples from the eighteen participating countries of the diversity of approaches to self-evaluation.[5] One of the most interesting aspects of the project is that, left to their own initiatives, schools have come up with their own approaches, surprising policy-makers (and often themselves) by their inventiveness and enthusiasm. For example, in a Finnish school students devised their own observation schedule and, after negotiation with teachers, used it over a seven-week period to observe lessons (unannounced to teachers) and to make recommendations on learning and teaching. Their focus was particularly on classroom atmosphere as conducive to learning and help for slower learners. Staff were reported as being very positive because they already had three years' experience of evaluating the management and leadership skills of their headteacher. This school has developed an ongoing exchange with a network of schools in Ireland to share ideas on tools and processes of self-evaluation. The Irish have set up a website to exchange ideas on school review.[6]

THE PACIFIC RIM

It is not only in Europe that self-evaluation has assumed a high priority. It is on the agenda in countries in virtually every continent. The Hong Kong government has invested heavily in consultation and exchange with countries around the world and has developed what might be called, in Alvik's terminology, a 'sequential' system. A set of performance indicators, developed by the Education Department, is circulated to schools. These cover four broad areas – management and organisation; teaching and learning; support for students and school ethos; and attainment and achievement. Schools are invited to supplement these with their own school-based indicators and assess their own performance using guidelines on roles and procedures published by the Education Department. The external quality assurance process starts with a pre-inspection, based on information supplied by the school, including questionnaire data from students, teachers and parents. There is a preparatory visit and meeting with parents before the inspection begins.

In Thailand similar intelligence gathering has been in progress for the last few years. After centuries of received wisdom, says the secretary-general of the National Education Ministry, they are looking to a more bottom-up approach to evaluation and development. Save the Children and UNICEF are both involved in supporting pilot work with schools and there are impressive examples of teacher-directed self-evaluation involving pupils in the building and revising of databases which include pupils' attainments, attitudes to learning and teaching and parent feedback to the school.

ISRAEL

Israel provides an excellent example of a thorough systematic sequential model. It starts with seventy to eighty hours of basic training in programme evaluation, testing out data collection and data analysis. Participating schools then establish internal evaluation teams of three or four teachers who have attended the training workshops. This integral evaluation team chooses a focus for evaluation as a test run of their expertise, with technical support from an external tutor. After this, the internal evaluation team is institutionalised as a permanent feature of the school. The composition of the team changes periodically so that all interested teachers have a chance to participate in school evaluation. The team continues to receive technical assistance. When the school feels it is ready, external evaluation takes place.

The lessons the Israelis have learned, as described by Nevo, are:

- School people understand best the meaning of evaluation through distinctions between description and judgement
- Students and their achievements should not be the only object of school evaluation
- Outcomes or impact should not be the only thing looked at when evaluating
- School evaluation has to serve both formative and summative functions, providing information for planning and improvement as well as certification and accountability
- There is no meaningful way to judge the overall quality of a school by one single criterion or a universal combination or multiple-type criteria
- Internal evaluation can best be served by a team of teachers for whom evaluation is only part of their job definition, supported by appropriate training and expert external assistance
- To make it meaningful, it is necessary to mobilise many alternative tools and methods of inquiry
- Learning by doing is still the best way to learn how to conduct evaluation
- Internal evaluation is a prior condition to useful external evaluation

Nevo concludes:

A school that does not have an internal mechanism for self-evaluation will have difficulties in developing positive attitudes towards evaluation, and lack the self-confidence necessary for constructive dialogue between the school and the external evaluation. In such cases, evaluation becomes a source of accusations and defensiveness rather than a basis for dialogue between internal and external decision makers.[7]

NORTH AMERICA

In North America there is an ongoing search to find the optimum balance between quality and accountability, between top-down and bottom-up, internal and external evaluation. At federal level the policy agenda is dominated by concerns of national standards and indicators of international performance. At state or provincial level, however, there is an interesting mosaic of practice.

In Quebec Province, for example, the Ministry of Education publishes extensive data on school performance, including comparisons at provincial level and comparative data on the performance of Quebec Province and French school students. In parallel, the Ministry publishes a self-assessment pack for schools containing questionnaires and other survey instruments for teachers, students and management that covers a wide range of features of school life. The instruments were derived from a research study involving 6,500 students and 1,600 teachers in francophone schools. At the same time, a quite separate pilot project was being carried out at McGill University with the English-speaking Quebec schools. The 'Schools Speaking to Stakeholders' project came to very similar conclusions about the importance of the stakeholder perspective in self-evaluation but came to it by a different route.[8] Like 'Schools Speak for Themselves', the McGill study built from the ground up, with the close involvement of classroom teachers from the outset.

On the opposite coast of Canada, British Columbia has developed an approach which is close to Alvik's sequential model. Its title, 'Building Excellence Together', is an apt description of its purposes and underlying values. The BC Ministry of Education provides schools with an 'accreditation manual', taking them through the process of self-evaluation and including survey and questionnaire instruments on school culture, staff development, school and community, leadership and learning. This school-based evaluation provides the basis for a visit by an external assessment team. Their task, as laid out in the manual, is to meet with staff and engage in dialogue on strengths and areas for change, to give both support and challenge to the school's growth plan and agree on how the outcomes would be reported to the wider community.

The United States presents an even more colourful patchwork of different approaches. Later in this chapter James Learmonth describes some of the challenges of a self-evaluation approach in Chicago. The 'School Inquiry Project' is particularly interesting, involving schools in presenting their 'digital portfolio', a CD-ROM interactive showcase compiled by students and teachers, with students leading the way in software design.

AUSTRALIA

Sequential models, similar to the British Columbia model, can be found in Australia. In Victoria the 'Schools for the Future' programme uses a process of independent, external school review but takes as its focus the school charter, a document drawn up by the school itself that contains its profile, its priorities and its code of practice. The review and renewal of the charter on a three-yearly cycle, with external guidance, is seen as providing schools with the support and challenge to improve their performance in a systematic way. An important component of this was the parents' questionnaire which, as defined by the Ministry of Education, helped to:

- identify areas for improvement
- identify trends and patterns which emerge from regular surveys
- monitor the school's performance against its own goals
- demonstrate publicly standards of achievement reached by the school

In New South Wales school profiles are compiled by schools themselves and provide the basis for quality assurance and external review. The school profile contains information on:

- the socio-economic background of the school (statistical and descriptive)
- school population, numbers and distribution of students and teachers
- attendance data – patterns by different year groups
- attainment data for the last year
- trends in attainment over time
- results of surveys of parents, students and staff.

A WORLD-WIDE MOVEMENT

There are countries throughout the world seeking to find the optimum balance of internal and external evaluation. In Argentina in October 1998 the Ministry of Education brought together twenty-three Latin American countries to explore self-evaluation with three specific foci – evaluation and educational policy; evaluation and school improvement; and evaluation and public information. For all countries present from Central and South American as well as the Iberian Peninsula, these were the three major challenges to the development of internal/external evaluation – that is, recognising that the accountability and policy development dimensions are closely allied to the essential, school-improvement purpose of evaluation.

In the former Soviet republics there is a long road to the rebuilding of national systems but many of those republics – including Georgia, Kyrgyzstan and Uzbekistan – are looking to European expertise to help in the construction of systems of evaluation. In Uzbekistan, for example, teachers are currently evaluated on a five-yearly cycle but without an underpinning infrastructure of agreed criteria, tools of evaluation or stakeholder involvement. Drawing on a 'Schools Speak for Themselves' approach, the Ministry of Education is currently piloting a more bottom-up approach to school and teacher self-evaluation involving a pilot scheme in seventeen schools using questionnaires for pupils, parents and teachers.

Discussing the relationship between a bottom-up approach and a top-down approach in the Seychelles, Vidot highlights the dangers of 'a regulatory system of quality control' being seen by policy-makers as more expedient than one 'geared to encouraging and supporting school-based evaluation'.[9] He also offers a warning about 'accountability as vindication of the system'. If measures are used and indicators developed to service a political purpose, schools will not grow into genuine learning organisations. As in many other parts of the world, the Seychelles are consulting widely and proceeding cautiously to find the optimum balance.

SCOTLAND

The Scottish approach may be described as being in a stage of transition from a parallel to a sequential model with a vision of what a genuinely co-operative approach might look like in the future. It has come a long way in less than a decade.

In 1992 the Scottish Office Education Department made a radical change in its approach to the evaluation of schools. Criteria of inspection were made public for the first time and indicators and guidelines for their use were published for the first time.[10] This document was described by Her Majesty's Chief Inspector Archie McGlynn as an 'opening of the secret gardens of the Inspectorate'. As director of the Audit Unit, he commissioned research which would lead to a framework of indicators derived from the expectations of teachers, parents and pupils. There was, at that time, a considerable degree of scepticism about the value of asking people, and pupils in particular, about the quality of their schools. Concerns were expressed that disaffected students would see it as an opportunity to be abusive or to get back at their teachers. Some headteachers argued that they already knew what teachers, parents and pupils thought about the school.

Fears were dispelled when teachers saw the nature of the feedback and found that young people took the exercise seriously and acted responsibly. Often the data confirmed what people already knew. Praise for good teachers was no surprise, nor was it news to hear about the state of the toilets, the quality of food or lack of lockers. However, there were always new insights, revelations about the secret harmonies and hidden discords in the underlife of the school, the new angles of insight into age-old problems. The positive and insightful nature of students' comments continues to surprise schools seven years down the line. In that time, schools have become more adventurous and risk-taking, finding ways of getting more detail, more specific information and more penetrating ways of gathering data on the effectiveness of learning and teaching.

It took the vision and courage of HMCI McGlynn and his colleagues to move in such a radical direction but it was rooted deeply in a conviction that when people are trusted and allowed ownership they will gratify and surprise. A system engaged in such a radical transition has both fast- and slow-moving currents. Now some schools are at the cutting edge of self-evaluation while a few have hardly begun to move. The same would hold true, to some extent, for individual inspectors. While working to a common protocol and clear centrally directed guidelines, some inspectors would incline more to the parallel model – 'inspecting' a school with minimal account of the school's own self-evaluation. A more advanced inspection team would be closer to the sequential model, building on the school's own internal work, while at the progressive end would lie a more co-operative, negotiated approach.

While Alvik's classification is a typology rather than a taxonomy – it does not necessarily imply a progression from one type to the next – the school-improvement evidence suggests that, as a school system matures, it moves in a progressive line from external inspection, through parallel evaluation, to sequential and co-operative models. Following this argument, the English and Welsh systems would be characterised at national level as, at best, a 'parallel' one, but at local authority level these are examples of sequential and co-operative models in force or in the process of development.

The influence of 'School Speak for Themselves' in aiding this progression has not been restricted to the United Kingdom, as the following two case studies show. They provide an interesting contrast. The Chicago example illustrates how, within a top-down system, a more bottom-up approach can bring a new vitality to the work of teachers. The Danish example suggests that, in a system without formal evaluation of any kind, it may be possible to build from the ground up.

A Chicago approach

James Learmonth

Teachers in UK schools who are frustrated in their desire to speak for themselves should not assume that things are any better in US cities such as Chicago. The success of schools there is judged almost exclusively on the basis of students' test scores and a severe system of remediation and probation is in place for those schools whose test scores are judged to be too low. A city teacher's main pre-occupation is to get student scores up. In some schools teacher confidence is further challenged by 'direct instruction', a system of tightly scripted lessons where opportunities for teachers to use their imagination or professional judgement in how they teach are sharply reduced. Opportunities for reflection and self-evaluation have also been rare.

Within this context of pressure for urgent and measurable reform, the 'School Change and Inquiry Programme', led by former HMI David Green and funded by the MacArthur Foundation, has been working with twenty-four elementary and high schools in order to develop their strategies and skills into inquiring into three specific areas:

- teaching and learning
- student learning, progress and achievement
- schools as learning communities

Through engaging with each school, the programme supports the school in providing a considered and accurate account of its work – 'a telling of its own story', as David Green puts it.

'Schools Speak for Themselves' has been one of the key texts in working with Chicago schools in the programme. With such a high priority given to increasing test scores and so much change demanded from both institutions and individuals, it has been difficult to find time for the commitment to critical and systematic reflection on practice as a basis for individual and collective development. Not that teachers in Chicago are unwilling. When given the opportunity to reflect, whether at workshops or in other forums, during school visits, they have been eager to contribute and to learn. Working with the support of critical friends, they have been keen to develop the vocabulary and concepts with which to discuss their practice.

Observing other teachers' lessons, as in the UK, is a particularly sensitive area, though the idea of peer coaching is well established in some schools. But without a tradition of inspection to provide the concepts and vocabulary of evaluation, American teachers are often initially uncomfortable with the idea of school self-evaluation. It is seen as another potential source of negative criticism. School principals, unlike many headteachers in the UK, tend to be seen more as administrators than as curriculum leaders – so who are they to make judgements on teaching and learning in the classroom? If principals, or other administrators, visit a classroom, surely they must be there to check on the performance of an individual teacher. And, anyway, what evidence is there that a school has a coherent or explicit common understanding of what 'effective practice' is?

Teachers in the programme have worked enthusiastically in developing their capacity to reflect on and evaluate the school's performance, often using the framework provided by 'Schools Speak for Themselves'. An unusual aspect of the programme is the school's commitment to 'Schools Speak for Themselves' through an individual Digital School Portfolio, which is a careful and considered compilation of the school's work. The DSP highlights both accomplishments and challenges and makes these accessible to a range of potential audiences through the use of modern interactive technologies. Chicago's citizens will have an opportunity to see and hear the schools' stories at an exhibition early in 1999.

Chase Elementary School is one of the schools most closely involved in the programme. It has regularly sent teachers to the workshops, and, shortly after a new principal was appointed, welcomed the opportunity for members of the SCIP team to carry out a review of the school's current performance, concentrating particularly on the quality of teaching and learning, the assessment of student work, and the school as a learning community. The report of the review was written in a sharp, constructive and accessible style which stimulated much staff discussion, reflection and action in the subsequent weeks and months.

The staff were also invited to add an appendix to the written report which was the outcome of a day's in-service training. The first part of the day was spent with a member of the SCIP team working with the entire staff, in plenary and in small groups, analysing different aspects of what 'Schools Speak for Themselves' describes as the ten indicators of a good school. Later, teachers first worked in year groups to answer a specific question and a related follow-up question:

- What are the characteristics of a classroom which gives top priority to improving student achievement?
- What are the characteristics of a school which gives top priority to improving student achievement?

This was followed by a plenary session involving feedback from the groups, some debate, suggested amendments or developments, some further input from the SCIP team member and a general agreement about a final summary of the day's work. The culmination was a set of agreed criteria and three sets of guidelines – one for students, one for teachers and one for school management. Some examples of the 'should', drawn from extensive lists, are given below.

Students should:

- be involved in classwork, group work and individual work
- have the chance to learn independently through discovery
- have opportunities to take the initiative
- have access to a computer/learning centre
- have an active role in the way the class is run

Teachers should:

- be aware of individual students' learning needs
- have high expectations of students
- give positive reinforcement
- constantly assess student progress
- give each student some one-to-one time
- offer alternative problem-solving strategies to students
- be able to move between facilitating, directing, coaching, etc.
- show that they love what they are doing

Administrators should:

- support staff in making learning the top priority
- provide an atmosphere where teachers feel comfortable, confident, trusted and where they get constructive criticism
- talk with students as part of the observation time
- give teachers opportunities to observe other teachers in Chase and elsewhere
- sustain an open-door policy for questions, suggestions, problems
- model good teaching

What the teachers at the school had done in collaboration was to take a further step along the road of exploring collective wisdom to enable the construction of a widely shared framework for school self-evaluation.

A Danish approach

Lejf Moos, Mette Lovbjerg, Lise Tingleff Nielsen, Johnny Thomassen, Peter Ulholm, CLUE, Research Centre for School Leadership, School Development and School Evaluation at the Royal Danish School of Educational Studies

Two years ago we became very inspired by the model of school evaluation described in 'Schools Speak for Themselves'. We liked the idea that evaluation is always based on a set of values that are articulated and discussed by the participants in school life. We also liked the idea that the school should open itself up to parents and the local community and involve them in the evaluation processes. And we liked the notion that pupils should have a voice in the valuing and evaluation of the school too.

The Danish school system has, as in the United Kingdom, experienced a flurry of decentralisation and new public management, but the ways in which the Danish government has applied the principles in restructuring the educational system are different from the British. The devolution of financial management of schools in 1991 gave powers to the local authorities (the communes), letting them, if they wished, devolve further to each and every individual school. At the same time, parents were given more power through school boards, although only in an advisory role.

While there are some tendencies towards greater centralised control of the curriculum, this trend has not been nearly as strong as in the United Kingdom. The Danish school system has no national standards of performance (as yet), nor inspections by national or local authorities. For many years, Danish teachers were considered professional and autonomous both in their choice of methodology and selection of curriculum content, provided they stuck to national and local guidelines. In other words, there was a kind of invisible contract between the teachers and school leaders whereby management was handed over to the leader as long as he or she did not interfere with teachers' decisions about curriculum content and methods of teaching. Parental co-operation was very strong at classroom level and with respect to individual children.

Given that teachers are unaccustomed to any form of external control, it is difficult for many of them to get used to the new demands for accountability and transparency in school and classroom practice. Nonetheless, these are written into the Act of 1993 which makes the school leader responsible for the planning and evaluation of the teachers' teaching. This means, of course, that there have to be ways of finding this out. By the same token, if schools are to be held accountable to parents and local authorities for the performance of the pupils and students, there need to be valid forms of assessment and evaluation. To this end, the Ministry of Education has initiated two major projects to develop new tools and procedures for evaluating pupil performance, classroom teaching and other school-related activities. One of the two projects is called the 'Four Cities Project: School Development through School Evaluation'. In each city three schools are participating, supported by external consultants from the Royal Danish School of Educational Studies. We are working in four schools in one of these cities, Copenhagen.

The Copenhagen Model

The basic idea of The Copenhagen Model is that evaluation is an integrated part of school development. In this, as in the NUT model, teachers, pupils and parents are seen as stakeholders with the right to a voice in the functioning and improvement of the school.

In each school, there is a developmental committee made up of school leader, teachers and school board representatives (after much discussion, schools decided against having pupils on the committee, due to the nature of the work in steering, co-ordinating and planning). A lot of managerial power is invested in this committee and it is seen as pivotal to proceedings. One principal duty for this committee is to make sure that discussions are carried out within the groups which they represent.

Stage one in our model is the discussion of values. Teachers, pupils and parents are asked for their answers to the question: what is a good school? The next stage is to ask the same participant, and again initially individually, to sort out a set of cards with statements as to what a good school should be or do. After choosing ten out of twenty cards, the participants are asked to put them into order of priority. The next stage is again to form groups and ask them to agree within the groups on the order of priority of cards.

Some of the statements written on the cards were:

- pupils are listened to
- the school welcomes differences between pupils as a strength of the school
- all pupils have equal opportunity of getting praise
- the school is sensitive to the social, cultural and linguistic background of its pupils
- co-operation with parents is important for pupils' performance in school

What came out of these two exercises provided the starting point for designing questionnaires which would help in reflecting back to the school its priorities and values and provide a basis for making comparisons between schools. Four different questionnaires were devised – one for teachers, one for parents, one for pupils (kindergarten class to class four) and one for students (classes five to ten).

On the adult and student questionnaires each statement had to be answered twice: on the left-hand side in terms of importance – how important is this? – and on the right-hand side in terms of current performance – how good is our school on this aspect?

The questionnaire for the younger pupils asked the same kind of questions but in a simpler design where they were asked to draw some of their answers if they wished.

Schools were innovative in getting returns to the questionnaires. In one school pupils were promised fizzy drinks if all the parents in their class returned the questionnaires. In another school there was a drawing of lots for a basket with fruits and wine among the parents returning the questionnaires. In both schools the number of parents returning questionnaires was high!

Responses were processed by the consultants and fed back first to the developmental committees or to all teachers, depending on each school's choice. This gave impetus to the discussion of priorities and performance. Responses were looked at in four ways, a fairly time-consuming exercise:

- What are the views of a specific group of stakeholders?
- Where were the biggest gaps between 'what is' and 'what ought to be'?
- Where do groups agree and where are there wide discrepancies?
- Where did different groups agree with each other and on what did they disagree?

Summaries and recommendations were put together either by the school committee or by the consultants. The following is a short extract from a report in one school:

Theme 3: The climate for learning

Younger pupils communicate well with teachers. But they are not sure what they are good at and they don't experience much room for participation.

Parents think that more could be done to promote the effectiveness of pupils' learning in order to make use of all their potential. They think that teachers should listen more to pupils' points of view. Teachers don't think it is important that students should have a say on the planning of teaching. However, teachers do not agree among themselves on what constitutes good teaching and good learning and they do not discuss on a regular basis how to promote learning opportunities for their pupils' learning.

The consultants' recommendations:

- you should try to involve the pupils in the discussion of content and form of teaching
- as a group of teachers you should discuss the way you view children in this school
- time and space should be made, experiment with different approaches to teaching and learning and discussion of what makes for 'good' teaching and learning

Later on parents and members of the school board were invited to listen to and discuss the same feedback. Parents found the picture of the school that emerged a credible and recognisable one but were surprised by the somewhat negative attitude of the teachers. The school board was surprised that its contribution to school improvement was not valued by the teachers. This led to a fruitful two-day seminar involving board members and teachers.

Out of this, schools developed action plans, choosing different areas for specific focus such as teaching and learning, teambuilding and teamworking, parent–school co-operation, with pupils' participation being the most common choice of focus. In different ways, all teachers in all schools became involved in one developmental project or the other. A very important cornerstone of the Copenhagen Model is that evaluation is seen as only part of a longer-term process.

Having run through the exercise with the first set of schools, we learned a lot which helped us to revise the approach the second time around.

- opportunities to express differences in opinions are important; if the statements are too 'soft', there is a tendency for the consensus to give too rosy a picture
- the time span in the process from discussing values to the evaluation should not be too long; people forget or lose interest.
- the amount of data should be limited in order that it may be dealt with in a specific and focused way
- teachers should play an integral part in the process from evaluation to action

However, our first version of the cards seemed to signal the 'right' kind of school and we felt there was a tendency to choose the 'politically correct' response. While providing the 'correct' kind of picture, we felt that it did not produce enough material and energy to invest in further action. We also wanted to get more specific and fine-grained criteria on learning and teaching.

So, next time round with a new set of ten schools, we made a number of changes. We focused less on the school and put pupil learning more to the fore. So our starting point was with:

- what should the pupils learn?
- how should the pupils learn?
- the school's view of children
- co-operation between school and parents
- the school's social and the pedagogical climate
- the school's image
- the school's frames
- school-based leisure-time activities

Statements in the card sort exercise were derived from these categories, including some provocative statements in order to stimulate debate and discussion instead of promoting an immediate consensus.

It is important to find what values and assessments are really behind the picture that parents, pupils and professionals have of the school; the interplay and interference between school culture; the values and routines of the professional participants of school life (and partly the pupils); and the image of the school, the pictures, the reputations, the opinions of the parents (and partly of the pupils). It is only in analysing this interplay that one can find the school's identity – the centre of the life and development of the school.

The answers we got from the second-generation schools suggested we had been right in tightening the focus. Firmer, bolder statements emerged. The closer involvement of teachers during the whole exercise has made the processing of the material easier. We now have the same categories for all groups, which makes it much easier to compare answers from parents with those from pupils and teachers.

In our revised model discussions with pupils in classes one to six were carried out by the teachers. Pupils wrote down, or drew, their opinions with a follow-up discussion in class managed by the teacher. This led to the formulation of ten statements agreed by the teacher and the class. Teachers expressed great satisfaction with this procedure because it gave them the opportunity to discuss these issues with their own pupils, allowing them to incorporate these insights into their teaching.

So what we lose in openness and the broad horizons, we have gained in a process which brings us closer to the actual practice of evaluation and development.

9

A FRAMEWORK FOR
SELF-EVALUATION

The end point of our 1995 study was a framework for self-evaluation which could be used by schools and authorities for quality assurance and school improvement. This chapter describes the key elements of a framework.

What do we think of when we hear or see the word 'framework'? We are likely to picture something that holds things together, an outer shell or scaffolding. A self-evaluation framework should have that character. It should provide a structure giving shape and coherence to what would otherwise be a loose conglomeration of good ideas and interesting practices. However, it should neither come ready-made nor be delivered in a flatpack with a blueprint for self-assembly because this leads to deskilling and, in an educational context, to the deprofessionalisation of teachers.

The 'Schools Speak for Themselves' study taught us something important about frameworks. They are an end point rather than a starting point. They evolve from discrete parts into a coherent whole, and it is the process of evolution that gives them shape and meaning. To be useful in a way which respects and enhances teachers' professionalism, a framework has to find the point of balance between prescription and broad principles. It should not require teachers to reinvent the wheel but nor can it offer simple answers to complex issues. What follows, therefore, should be seen more as the guiding principles of a framework than a neat and tidy set of prescriptive steps.

Our framework for self-evaluation has four key elements:

- an overarching philosophy
- procedural guidelines
- a set of criteria or 'indicators'
- a tool kit

A PHILOSOPHY

A philosophy is, in this context, a set of beliefs. These are unashamedly value judgements about people, about relationships, about learning, about organisations, about what makes people want to be teachers and what makes them want to go on teaching, even when children are at their most disinterested. Because a philosophy is essentially about values and value judgements, it is neither precluded from being intrinsically 'good', nor from being good science. It will be said by historians in the future that as human beings entered the third millennium, they took with them an immense store of knowledge about themselves and the keys to their own evolution, all too often ignored and unused.

So, however philosophical in nature, the first element of the framework is also grounded in evidence. It draws on the collective wisdom of teachers. It reflects the decades of work of social scientists. It respects the accumulated wisdom of great minds and is validated by the work of neuropsychologists and biologists who can now provide physiological evidence about the inner workings of intuition, motivation, emotion, thinking and learning. It also benefits from insights from quantum physics, chaos and complexity theory which illustrate natural laws of organisations and further our understanding of 'unnatural' organisations such as schools.

The key tenets of the philosophy are:

- human beings are natural learners
- development and change come from within
- feedback is critical to individual learning and to organisational development
- people have a commitment to that which they themselves have created

Learning sits at the very centre of the philosophy. Learning is what schools are there to promote. They are most effective in that endeavour when school learning is pursued in conjunction with home learning and with other sources of understanding which pupils bring with them. Learning builds on prior knowledge and experience. Learning is multifaceted and engages all the senses and intelligences. It is enhanced when it is mediated through other people – adults, parents, peers and teachers. Intellectual growth is social and emotional in origin and thrives in a supportive, gregarious climate.

However, schools do not simply exist to promote the achievements of a cohort of pupils who pass through them at any given time. Schools serve children and young people over generations and have long-term aims. They invest in the future as well as serving the present and must therefore be learning centres, laboratories in which teachers continually enhance and upgrade their skills. They are a resource for parents and the immediate community, are 'beacons' for other schools to learn from. They have a role in the development of policy, practice and new ideas. Nationally, and often internationally, they are the generators of knowledge and the engines of reform. Systems only grow and improve through the cutting-edge practice in their schools. All significant and lasting change is ultimately teacher-led.

This does not happen without support from the outside, from professional associations, authorities, colleges and universities. Schools need systems of support, challenge and advocacy with the primary purpose of helping them build on good practice and learn from the experiences of others. They deserve the well-informed and sensitive challenge of critical friends, provided through advisory, review or 'inspection' systems.

All of the schools in our 1995 study wanted to improve aspects of their present practice. This was generally true of pupils as well as of teachers, and every parent we spoke to wanted to see evidence of growth and progress in their children. At the same time, all groups of stakeholders wanted reassurance about the things they were presently doing well as teachers, headteachers, parents or pupils. All groups welcomed the support as well as the challenge from outside but only when they could see the integrity of its purpose.

For our framework to be real and credible to teachers, it should, therefore, carry with it the conviction that it comes from 'real' schools, not derived from abstract criteria, nor presented as a 'counsel of perfection'. The framework has to be 'inclusive', clearly signalling its respect for a broad base of opinions – from teachers, pupils, parents, governors, support staff and others. By observing these principles, it lays the groundwork for procedures, criteria and tools of evaluation.

PROCEDURAL GUIDELINES

The second element of the framework is to set out the procedures and sequences of actions that are most likely to help realise the vision and underwrite success. These are not tablets of stone but they draw on a substantial body of research into professional and organisational development and come from our own school-improvement work in a number of different national contexts and cultures. Guided by the philosophy and its cardinal principles, the procedural guidelines are given below.

First, start with the end in mind

Starting with the end in mind is a first principle of evaluation. The question is where will it take you and why do you want to go there? It is important to be clear and honest about reasons for engaging in the exercise and to recognise what are 'good' reasons, as opposed to pragmatic and judicious ones. Pragmatic reasons are essentially about micro-politics and may be advocated because the school will ultimately be the beneficiary. Good reasons are those with an essentially educational purpose. The following might all be compelling reasons for engaging in self-evaluation; some are intrinsically educational in nature and some pragmatic; most are inter-related:

- there is an impending inspection
- it is authority policy
- it will help to counteract negative media reporting
- it will provide feedback to teachers
- it will strengthen the self-improvement capacity of the school
- it will enhance the professionalism of staff
- it will help to make learning more effective
- it will increase the effectiveness of management and leadership
- it may help to attract resources or sponsorship
- it will provide information to attract new parents

While self-evaluation should be embarked upon primarily because it will benefit pupils and support teachers, these purposes do not have to be in conflict with the pragmatic and political ones. However, if self-evaluation is driven solely by political motives, unaccompanied by a genuine commitment to its educational value, it will be an empty and cynical exercise. It is important, therefore, to consider what different groups of stakeholders are going to get out of the exercise. What is in it for teachers, pupils and parents? Who is the evaluation for? Who is the end user or 'audience' of the information?

In practice, there are likely to be multiple audiences, some internal to the school and some external. People will want different things from the evaluation and will seek outcomes that are most likely to meet their needs and fit their own priorities. But evaluation can also take people beyond these immediate concerns. It can extend their horizons so that next time round they are looking further and asking more challenging questions.

When people are aware of the eventual outcome, they can see how it will feed into developments at school, classroom or departmental level. In these days of bland mission statements and targets, those generated through a process of self-evaluation will be seen as a more useful and relevant road to 'quality' than those apparently arbitrary goals and targets derived from a distant database.

Self-evaluation starts with three questions for the five-year-old at the very beginning of his or her school life:

- What am I good at?
- What can I get better at?
- Who can help?

These are the same three questions for the teacher, for managers and for administrators. For the school itself, these also provide the starting point for evaluation. The three questions at school level are:

- What are we (as a school) good at?
- What can we get better at?
- Who can help?

These layers of self-reflection – individual, organisational, leadership – were portrayed by a Danish cartoonist.[1]

Diagram 9.1 Layers of self-reflection (illustration by Allan Stocholms)
Source: *Folkeskolen*, the Danish Teachers' Weekly Magazine

A study by two American researchers identified three important factors in determining whether a person would be motivated in their work or their learning.[2] These can also be seen as applying at each layer within the school:

- experienced meaningfulness – 'the extent to which a person perceives work as being worthwhile or important, given his or her system of values'.
- experienced responsibility – 'the extent to which a person believes that he or she is personally responsible or accountable for the outcomes of efforts'.
- knowledge of results – 'the extent to which a person is able to determine on a regular basis whether or not the outcomes of his or her efforts are satisfactory'.[3]

Starting with the end in mind means seeing these criteria as the desired end point of evaluation – an integral aspect of management and of teaching. These demanding criteria can also become embedded in the thinking of pupils and may extend to parents too.

Second, create the climate

Climate is all. Self-evaluation can only work when there is a climate for it and when the conditions are right. The research literature, as well as the day-to-day experiences of teachers, tell us that self-evaluation requires a climate of trust and an openly agreed agenda. It needs the willing participation of people, with a clear and unambiguous agreement about purposes and outcomes. This is a sine qua non and from it flows some practical considerations.

- The surroundings for the process should be familiar and reassuring. For example, if parents use a particular 'drop-in' room, then the discussions can take place there. The staff room may be more congenial than the school lecture theatre. Facilities for publicly recording agreement (for example, flip charts, paper and pens) should be available.
- It should build on existing forums – for example, governors' meetings, PTA evenings, departmental/stage meetings. INSET days, for example, may be a good starting point before moving on to mixed groups.
- Small comforts such as a cup of coffee and a soft chair can make the surroundings less formal without detracting from the importance of the task.
- The more people involved in the climate setting and planning, the more it will gain its own momentum. Decisions about where and how to go about it should allow people to make suggestions, offer help and take responsibility for different aspects of the exercise.

Self-evaluation has to be set in a developmental context. The starting point should be with where the school currently is in its thinking and development. Decisions about the best way forward should take into account the amount of time people feel they can legitimately devote to this activity at any given point in the school year. As soon as it is perceived as a burden, or as being imposed from the outside, it will lose its impact.

In planning the exercise account has to be taken of other cycles in the school year. If the process is likely to build on, rather than interfere with, existing structures and in-school processes (for example, stage planning/evaluation; team/departmental meetings), then it should:

- be incorporated well in advance into existing planning cycles
- be negotiated with the various groups
- build in time for reflection as well as action

Third, promise confidentiality

When there is confidentiality, people feel freer to comment honestly and without inhibition on aspects of school life which are important to them. It should be made clear from the outset that it will not be possible to identify the source of the information. It should be explained that data will be aggregated and show general trends rather than expose individuals. Where disaggregation is used (for example, breaking data down by gender or age) this can only be done where there are sufficiently large numbers to make it valid or to respect confidentiality. Procedures, such as sealed envelopes or posting boxes, give people confidence in the integrity of the exercise.

Where there is open discussion on issues, the ground rules need to be clear so that no one feels vulnerable either in voicing an opinion or in being, apparently, the object of critical comment. The issues need to be presented in such a way as to focus on issues rather than individuals, on what can be changed and how the change can be managed. It should be about taking responsibility rather than apportioning blame.

Fourth, take a risk

Engaging in any public process of self-evaluation can be a risky business. Asking genuinely open questions may well result in unpalatable or challenging answers. The questions, once asked, raise expectations that something will happen and that improvement will result. And, of course, opening up issues to debate may give the disaffected a platform to be negative and carping. Senior management may be seen as 'fair game' by some while others may have hobby horses to ride. Finally, there may be some who are reluctant to engage in the process at all. The risk is that self-evaluation may become a destabilising process.

Many of these apprehensions will turn out to be unfounded and most can be avoided by planning, openness and by ensuring a supportive climate. Nonetheless, there will always be a certain element of risk. For the schools in this study, and other similar projects in Scotland, the risk proved to be acceptable to the schools involved, and although always challenging in some aspects, paved the way for progress and improvement. The risk factor should:

- be assessed and discussed beforehand
- be preceded by agreement on how issues will be tackled
- be accompanied by support structures.

Fifth, engage a critical friend

Reviewing yourself as an individual or as an organisation can be a threatening experience, especially where much has been invested and the need for success is strong. The contribution of an external agent can bring a measure of objectivity as well as a measure of support. It should not take away from the school's ownership of change but should assist the process in ways which the school feels to be appropriate. To be useful, a 'critical friend' must be someone with experience of school improvement and with expertise in working with a range of groups and in a variety of contexts. An expert critical friend can add immeasurably to the exercise.

The involvement of external facilitators can reduce any sense of threat by being able to employ a light touch, using activities such as brainstorming, card sorts or critical path analyses to create the right climate for self-evaluation. Perhaps the strongest argument for having a critical friend is that he or she can work with the school over time to assist in the process of change, bringing to the task experience of other schools and other approaches. The value of what Elliot Eisner calls the 'enlightened eye' comes from the accumulated wisdom of working with schools over a number of years:

> The ability to see what counts is one of the features that differentiates novices from experts . . . The expert knows what to neglect. Knowing what to neglect means having a sense for the significant and having a framework which makes the search for the significant efficient.[4]

This is, however, no authoritarian prescription for some kind of objective reality. The enlightened eye acknowledges the nature of individual insight and its always tentative nature:

> the way in which we see and respond and respond to a situation, and how we interpret what we see, will bear our own signature. This unique signature is not a liability but a way of providing individual insight into a situation.[5]

If critical friends are to be useful, they should be:

- credible in terms of their knowledge and experience of school self-evaluation processes
- able to get to know the school and its 'character'
- prepared to assist the school to ask challenging questions and offer advice and support in dealing with the answers

In behavioural terms he or she:

- seeks first to understand rather than seeking to be understood
- has a positive regard for the school and its community
- is encouraging and supportive

- helps people identify their needs and concerns
- helps people reflect critically on their own practice
- encourages the sharing of ideas
- pushes for evidence
- treats his/her own observations and judgements as one source of evidence, open to discussion and modification
- is himself/herself open to criticism
- is not afraid of conflict and handles it constructively
- refers people to useful sources of further information.

To give a greater sense of ownership and control, it is useful for the staff to draw up their own profile using a simple device, such as the following.

A critical friend

What we want from him/her	What we do not want from him/her

ESTABLISHING THE CRITERIA

At the heart of self-evaluation is a set of criteria. There are basically two ways of establishing these. One is to survey the large variety of sources that already exists and adapt these to your own context. The other is to replicate the process used in this study, deriving criteria from the key stakeholders in your own school.

Following the first approach entails knowing where to locate the sources and how to narrow the search and sift through those sources selectively and economic-ally. Many authorities have their own self-evaluation or self-review criteria and many are currently in the process of developing them. These are obviously a first point of reference. A good set of authority guidelines will not, however, claim to be exclusive and will encourage schools to consult other sources too. Room should be left for the initiative, creativity and ownership of the school itself.

Other sources that may prove useful are the Scottish Office publication 'How Good Is Our School?', the 'Guidelines for Investors in People' and the extensive list provided by Scheerens and Bosker in *Foundational Studies in School Effectiveness*.[6]

It is important that senior management or a delegated committee do not simply adopt someone else's set of indicators, passing them one further layer down a hierarchy. People should have a chance to talk them through or modify them, to attune them to local needs, context and colloquial use. Discussion and negotiation are an important part of the process.

The fifty indicators that we generated provide as sound a starting point as any, grounded as they are in a wide-ranging consultation. However, there is always a temptation to cut too quickly to the chase and to adopt criteria because they seem credible, appealing and seductively time-saving. Doing so, though, will almost inevitably leave some people behind, confused about the storyline and lacking any sense of involvement or engagement.

The second option is to replicate the process of the original NUT study. Three years on from that study, we have become more convinced of the value for a school of going through that exercise for themselves. In every school we have worked with, or heard from subsequently, taking time for reflection has helped to build a sense of engagement and ownership. People, whether parents, pupils, governors or teachers, were always glad to be asked and were consequently more inclined to maintain a long-term interest in developments. The more stakeholders are allowed to play a full part in the process, the more likely that strong relationships among the various groups will be forged, leading to action which is lasting and sustainable. It need not be disruptive or time-consuming and it is virtually guaranteed to be an enriching and challenging experience for the school.

THE TOOLKIT

The guiding principle here is to hold fast to what is important and not to be tempted into measuring only what is easily measurable. Nor should you yield to the temptation of using tools most immediately to hand. The things that are most important to you are likely to be the hardest to measure. This is where the critical friend earns his or her keep. He or she can help you to find, customise or invent the instruments for gathering information relevant to your area of focus.

Attempts to evaluate the school across fifty dimensions of its work will be a frustrating, and perhaps futile, exercise. The focus should be on a limited number of indicators, perhaps just one cluster. Support for teaching, for example, might provide a good starting point because it will interest and involve teachers and be seen to be addressing an issue of fundamental concern to them.

Gathering evidence is likely to involve a range of approaches. It will include quantitative and qualitative data. The value of the former is that it can give you the big picture, the big numbers, the trends over time. The latter provides the detail, the flesh on the bones, and may be most valuable in pointing you towards what needs to be done.

The most common forms of quantitative data are:

- attendance rates
- attainment levels (SATS, GCSE/Standard Grades, standardised attainment tests)
- attitude questionnaires

Guidance on how to collect and use those data can be gained from a number of sources, including the OFSTED publication *Evaluation Matters*. Qualitative data are sometimes amenable to being turned into numbers but they are often particularistic and specific and come in the form of written comments, comments made in individual or group interviews, drawings, photographs or video. Useful sources for this are the series of publications by the Consortium of Institutes for Development and Research in Education in Europe (CIDREE) and the European Commission's 'Guide to School Self-evaluation'. These materials suggest interesting alternatives to questionnaires, which are sometimes in danger of overuse and can provoke consumer resistance. Nonetheless, questionnaires can be useful instruments and can add immeasurable value when used well and sparingly. A good questionnaire should meet the twin tests of economy and power. That is, it should be brief and easy to use but contain items which generate good robust information. In design or adaptation of questionnaires a number of simple rules should be observed.

Customise the language

Customise the language so that it is familiar to the particular group of users for whom it is intended. It should be in everyday vocabulary and unambiguous in meaning. Language can be a particularly sensitive issue for pupils, especially younger ones. It is therefore worthwhile involving pupils in the framing of questions, or testing out questions on a small sample of young people before using the items more widely. Giving pupils scope to write freely as well allows them to express themselves in their own language. This can result in a directness and freshness of terminology, bringing with it new ways of seeing things.

Use available and hidden expertise

Use the expertise of people in the school or community. Most schools will have teachers, parents and governors with a range of different experiences and expertise. There will probably be some who have been involved in market research or sales promotion, people who are good at stimulating dialogue and others who are a fund of ideas on how to structure group discussions in imaginative and productive ways. There will be people who have little relevant experience but come to the exercise with creativity, energy and a willingness to learn. These people are not always in management positions, nor will they always be school staff. This may be a plus in that the process is then more likely to be seen as widely based and non-hierarchical. Using expertise wherever it can be found may be a first step in creating a real 'community of inquiry'.

Make time

Make time for people to engage with the exercise if it is to be taken seriously. Time, as was frequently shown in our study, is the most precious of resources and however much of it is given over to the process, it should be 'quality time'. It must be planned in advance, should not conflict with other priorities and should be seen by those involved to be appropriate to the task in hand. The amount of time available has to be sufficient to enable discussion to take place and for groups to explore issues fully and arrive at conclusions as appropriate. The activities engaged in should be non-threatening and fun to do, allowing time for discussion both of the meaning of terms used and of the outcomes which emerge. Value and engagement will benefit from a variety of forums for discussion – individual, small groups and plenary. Perhaps the most important session will be when the action to be taken is agreed, the roles of individuals allocated and the means of evaluating progress decided.

IN SUMMARY

A framework for self-evaluation has the following characteristics:

- its purpose is clear
- its focus is on priorities
- it is context sensitive
- it is economical
- it is powerful
- it brings various parts together into a coherent whole
- it is user friendly
- it is inclusive
- it is flexible
- it provides a model of how to do rather than what to do
- it has freedom within it to accommodate change
- it provides tools for the job
- its outcomes are discussable
- it is action-orientated
- it leads to individual, and school, improvement

10

MAKING IT WORK IN YOUR SCHOOL

The process we went through with the ten schools in the NUT study is one that a school can replicate for itself. It is fairly simple and straightforward and needs no outside help. However, the support and facilitation from a critical friend can both lighten the load and introduce the neutrality of an outsider who knows nothing of old scores, interpersonal histories and hidden agendas. There are five main steps to follow.

1 CREATE THE CLIMATE

Staff need to be clear about the benefits to them and to their school. They need an opportunity to discuss this openly but set within a positive 'can do/will do' ethos. Questions that need to be addressed are:

- Who is the evaluation for?
- Who will benefit?
- What will those benefits be?

2 AGREE A PROCESS

Generate criteria which can be used with comfort and confidence by teachers, parents, pupils and others. With the support of the critical friend, organise representative groups of pupils, parents and teachers (possibly *all* teachers, depending on the size of the school). For example: ten groups of five pupils; three to five groups of five parents; two to three groups of five teachers.

Draw up a timetable for groups to meet with the critical friend over the course of, say, two to three (not necessarily consecutive) days. The timetable might look something like Table 10.1, but it is important to agree times that are suitable to parents' working hours and the availability of teachers.

Each group has a common task.

Table 10.1 Timetable for groups to meet with the critical friend

Time	Monday	Thursday	Monday
9.00–9.45	Pupil group 1	Pupil group 5	Pupil group 8
10.00–10.45	Pupil group 2	Pupil group 6	Pupil group 9
11.00–11.45	Pupil group 3	Pupil group 7	Pupil group 10
1.00–2.00	Parent group 1	Parent group 2	Parent group 3
3.00–4.00	Teacher group 1	Teacher group 2	Teacher group 3

Step 1 What makes a school good?

Individually write down five things that for you make a school good. Children who have difficulty in writing can be helped by an older child. Parents can also work in pairs where one does the writing. Very young children can draw things they like and don't like about their school. (About five minutes, or up to fifteen for young children.)

Step 2 Pooling and agreeing

The group of five comes together with the critical friend. He/she leads a discussion in which they share what people have written. This may give up to twenty-five different criteria. The critical friend should write them on a flipchart to recognise them publicly and give them status. (About fifteen minutes.)

There is likely to be repetition and overlap. The next task (perhaps for the critical friend) is to bring these ideas together into a common core, as seen below.

School as a safe place

- you feel safe
- there is no bullying
- there are people to speak to if you are worried about something

An orderly and disciplined climate

- you get peace to do your work
- people don't muck about in class
- people don't interrupt you when you are trying to work

Support for learning

- teachers help you when you don't understand
- you get help when you are stuck
- your teachers know when you are having difficulties

Repeat the same process with the teachers and with parents. This gives, in total, three versions which can then be brought together and examined for common themes.

Step 3 Fitting the pieces together

The next step is an optional one but is worth considering as a way of firming up the exercise and seeing how bottom-up and the top-down meet.

Each group is given a set of cards (twenty to twenty-five in total). Each card has one short statement – drawn from OFSTED's framework or from local authority criteria, as shown in Diagram 10.1.

The group is seated around a table or they sit on the floor, spreading the cards out in front of them. The task for the group is to agree on:

- the five cards they consider most important
- the three cards they consider least important

The critical friend plays no part in this unless:

- people want help with explaining what words mean
- there are language difficulties
- the group is stuck
- people are being left out
- one person is dominating
- the group is agreeing too quickly without adequate discussion

After the decision has been made by the group (fifteen minutes or so), the critical friend joins them to seek explanations for their ranking, for inclusions and omissions. If the exercise is being conducted with a larger number of people (for example, five groups of five parents), cards can be stuck with Pritt Stick or double-sided Sellotape to a sheet of poster paper and put up on the wall. The task for the critical friend in this scenario is to identify consensus and differences across the groups. This generates a lively discussion as groups compare their rankings and the reasons for them. In the course of discussion a lot can be learned about

Diagram 10.1 Examples of cards which may be produced by a group

how people see the school as well as what they think is of primary and of lesser importance.

3 AGREE THE CRITERIA

After two days of work with the groups, there is a fairly large body of data. For example, on the model above with fifteen groups of five people, and each person with five choices, there is a potential for 375 indicators ($15 \times 5 \times 5$). These may be reduced to anything between ten and thirty core items with some extra individualised items. In addition, there may be fifteen sets of card sort priorities.

All these data need to be brought together, categorised and reduced to a workable number, identifying:

- the core common themes
- the themes that are specific to some groups and not to others

This analysis can be carried out for the school by the critical friend, or it can be done by members of school staff (a working party, say) or by a group of pupils.

A quantitative table like Table 10.2 can be drawn up to show the frequency of mentions by different groups.

Table 10.2 Quantitative table showing frequency of mentions by different groups

Criterion	Total	Parents	Teachers	Pupils
Safety and security	50	13	8	29
Kind/helpful/caring teachers	46	11	3	32
Discipline/orderly atmosphere	36	12	11	13
High achievement by pupils	31	9	12	10
Mutual respect – teachers and pupils	30	10	6	14

Common themes which run across all sets of stakeholders can then be identified together with specific themes which are of importance for only one group of stakeholders. This will give you something similar to the lists below.

Common themes

- the school is a safe place
- there is a good atmosphere in the school
- there is mutual respect between pupils and teachers
- the school is well managed
- teachers help with learning difficulties

Teachers

- staff development time is used effectively
- staff are supported by the head

Parents

- teachers let you know when your child is having difficulty
- parents feel welcome in the school

Pupils

- your friends help you with your work
- you get to use computers
- there are quiet places to work

The card sort activity might be similarly categorised.

The criteria may, as they stand, provide the complete and self-sufficient set of criteria for the school's self-evaluation. However, some further work may be needed in one or more of the following:

- Comparing criteria with other sets from research or from policy documents to ensure that nothing important is missing, bearing in mind, though, that other sources of evidence may not be important or relevant in your own school and should not be imported simply because they have been found to be relevant in other contexts.
- Tidying up the language, making it specific, accessible and meaningful but keeping as far as possible the freshness and 'bite' of the original. Care should be taken to ensure that it is *not* jargonised.
- Focusing on specific areas where criteria need to be unpacked further. If the school is to develop a learning culture, it is important to focus on classroom climate, and on the processes of learning and teaching.

The critical friend has an important role to play here in ensuring that the school does not settle too easily for the cosy or comfortable criteria but gives due consideration to more challenging criteria as well. He or she must be knowledgeable about learning and teaching and help the school in its focus on classroom learning and parental support.

Once the criteria have been agreed, they should be fed back to the staff to discuss and agree. Their ownership of the criteria is crucial if they are to make active use of them.

The end point should be a limited set of key areas (say ten to twelve), each of these with three to five specific indicators. The final set of criteria may look something like Table 10.3. These are simply examples and not a complete set, but when undertaken by the school, the exercise should generate a comprehensive set, a guiding framework for the school to refer to, to use and to adapt over time.

Table 10.3 Some possible elements in a set of criteria

Indicator cluster	Indicators
The physical environment	• the school is a safe place • the school is clean and tidy • pupils' work is displayed on the walls • classrooms are colourful, attractive and stimulating
The social environment	• there is mutual respect between teachers and students • there is no bullying • the school is drug free
The learning environment	• the level of work is appropriate • pupils work together and learn from one another • pupils develop skills for life after school • pupils take responsibility for their own learning
The professional ethos	• there are opportunities for staff to develop their knowledge and expertise • teachers work together and share good practice • teachers have opportunities to take initiatives and exercise leadership

4 DEVELOP THE TOOLKIT

The toolkit is made up of instruments which the school can use to evaluate itself against the criteria that it has agreed. A school might, for example, choose to evaluate itself across all of these areas. It is usually a more fruitful approach, however, to focus on one or two specific areas. The critical friend should encourage people to include learning and teaching as areas for more in-depth treatment.

The two approaches – general and specific – are not mutually exclusive, however. A broad-brush, whole-school overview might help to define which areas to focus on more closely.

The following are examples of two approaches – a broad brush and a specific focus. These may be used for different purposes, separately, or as sequential steps in the same process.

A broad-brush approach

In this example the school has taken its ten areas and put them into a simple form or 'profile' with a four-category rating, standing for: 4 = major strengths, 3 = strengths outweigh weaknesses, 2 = weaknesses outweigh strengths, 1 = major weaknesses. The layout is shown in Table 10.4.

The profile instrument is then used as follows.

Step 1

Groups of pupils, parents and teachers are brought back together. As before, they work in groups of five. Each person in the group receives a copy of the profile. They are given five minutes or so to go through the profile *individually* (no

Table 10.4 A profile with a four-category rating

Area	1	2	3	4
The physical environment				
The social environment				
The learning environment				
Professional ethos and development				
Home–school links				
Community relationships				
Achievement and progress				
Management and leadership				
Personal and social development				
Student destinations				

conferring) and rate their school 1 to 4 on each of the items. Younger children may need to be paired with older children and the items translated into more simple language. (Time: five minutes.)

Step 2

The critical friend brings the group together and asks them to agree a group rating, going through each item one at a time with a new blank group profile. Discussion takes place item by item until there is agreement. On some items people may agree to disagree. That is acceptable as long as the views have been aired and considered. (Time: thirty to forty minutes.)

Step 3 option

A further optional extension of this exercise is for each group to send two or three representatives to a combined group of parents, pupils and teachers and to complete another school profile.

The rules of engagement for the critical friend are:

- encourage people to argue their case
- encourage listening to other people's point of view
- encourage people to offer evidence for their view
- seek consensus based on argument and evidence
- do not let people give in too easily
- do not allow 'averaging' (e.g. adding up the 4s, 3s and 2s and getting a group average)

The school may choose to do this exercise with a totally different group of pupils, parents and teachers from those who generated the criteria. A case can be made for either approach.

A second, more quantitative approach is to put the specific criteria (not the ten broad areas but the individual indicators) into a questionnaire instrument as shown in Diagram 10.2.

The school now							The effective school			
1	2	3	4	5		1	2	3	4	5

Pupils enjoy going to school

Teachers have opportunities for
professional development

Homework is marked regularly
and feedback is given

Parents are kept informed about
their children's learning

There is mutual respect between
teachers and students

Note: 1 = strongly agree / crucial
2 = agree / very important
3 = uncertain / fairly important
4 = disagree / not very important
5 = strongly disagree / not at all important

Diagram 10.2 A quantitative approach puts the specific criteria into a questionnaire instrument

This questionnaire may contain anything between ten and fifty items. It may be used by teachers or by teachers and parents, or by all three groups. It will generate a great deal of data and thought must be given beforehand to:

- how much data the school wants
- how the data will be processed
- what will be done with it afterwards
- how the data will be used in school development planning and school improvement

Will it be used:

- to get a broad-brush picture across all aspects of the school?
- to focus specifically on certain areas – for example, learning and teaching?
- to identify issues for further investigation?
- to identify areas for action – short, medium and long term?

The following is an example of how a set of criteria suggested by teachers, parents and pupils can be easily turned into a questionnaire format. All items in this version are phrased positively. Many researchers would argue that it is better to make a proportion of the items negative. That can be easily done. Items are also arranged randomly rather than in cognate groups. That is deliberate in that it keeps the respondent alert and offers a way of cross-checking responses to similar items in different positions on the questionnaire form.

These are just some examples of possible items. The questionnaire might be made longer and more testing. However, there is virtue in something that can be completed in just a few minutes.

SUPPORT FOR TEACHING	strongly agree	agree	disagree	strongly disagree
The size of the classes ensures that effective teaching can take place				
School management is aware of what goes on in classrooms				
Bad behaviour is dealt with effectively				
Support for learning and teaching is at the heart of school policy and planning				
Parents support their children's learning				
Pupils show respect for teachers				
Time is given to things that are important				
There is an adequate level of resources for teaching purposes				
Staff respect one another's work				
Workload is distributed fairly among staff				
There is a strong common sense of purpose and direction among staff				
The headteacher is accessible				
Staff share problems in their teaching				
Achievements of teachers are recognised and rewarded				
Management takes time to listen to teachers' concerns				

The following example contains some general questions about school climate, relationships and support for learning that might be used by a number of different groups of respondents: for example, pupils, teachers, management, governors and parents. Different responses may then be compared and examined to see where consensus and differences lie.

THE SCHOOL	a lot like this school	quite like this school	not much like this school	not at all like this school
The school is a safe place				
Pupils and teachers respect one another				
Visitors feel welcome in the school				
The school is well thought of in the community				
There is little vandalism and graffiti				
Class sizes ensure that pupils get individual attention				
Pupils are well behaved and well mannered				
The school is willing to change and adapt the way it does things				
Pupils feel they are learning something worthwhile				
Pupils get help and support when they need it				
There is good leadership				
There is a good overall level of attendance				
All pupils are encouraged to reach their maximum potential				
Pupils are given responsibility for making the school a better place				
There is a sense of order and purpose which helps learning				

The following example comes from what pupils said about good teachers. It is in their language, but the language register is such that it can be used by a wide range of different people – pupils, governors, parents, or teachers for self-evaluation purposes or to see how their own perceptions compare with those of their pupils.

TEACHERS	true of nearly all teachers	true of most teachers	true of some teachers	true of only a few teachers
Like teaching				
Treat people equally				
Let pupils know how they are doing				
Are encouraging				
Make their subject interesting				
Listen to the opinions of young people				
Make allowances for pupils with problems				
Take time to explain things				
Don't give up on you				
Know how to help you when you don't understand the work				
Keep confidences				
Help you to feel self-confident				
Expect you to work hard and do well				

One, among many, possible uses of the instrument is to identify gaps between what people say they want (goals or targets) and what they see as the current practice as shown in Table 10.5.

If the same questions have been given to different groups, comparisons such as those in Table 10.6 may be made, demonstrating the importance of different perspectives and highlighting areas for further development.

Table 10.5 What teachers see as crucial and what they see as the current practice

Area	Crucial	The school now
Pupils enjoy going to school	100	71
Homework is marked regularly and feedback given	88	58
Parents are kept informed about their children's learning	85	51

Table 10.6 Different group comparisons

Area	Agree/strongly agree		
	Teachers	Parents	Pupils
Pupils enjoy going to school	60	78	68
Homework is marked regularly and feedback given	80	72	40
Parents are kept informed about their children's learning	74	66	71

5 FOCUS ON LEARNING AND TEACHING

In the process of evaluation and improvement, it is important that attention is paid to the broader aspects of school culture, setting the conditions for professional reflection and development. Issues of learning and teaching will be difficult to address if attention is not given to some of the basic issues of infrastructure and well-being.

Self-evaluation must move at some stage into a specific focus on learning. The particular context of the school, and the judgement of the critical friend, will help to identify the best time to address those issues. They may emerge from the very beginning or they may develop later.

Either following such an exercise or as an alternative to it, staff may decide that they want a more fine-grained set of criteria on, for example, learning and teaching. This gives them the opportunity to build on the set. One simple mechanism for this is for a teacher to give his/her class the activity shown in Diagram 10.3 (the 'force field'), either individually or in small groups.

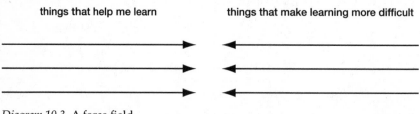

Diagram 10.3 A force field

This gives the teacher important feedback as well as helping to add detail to the indicator set. Results from one class are shown below.

Things that help

- telling you why you are learning something
- examples and stories which help you understand
- showing you how and where you went wrong and why
- the teacher can control the class
- helping you learn in different ways
- letting you set targets for yourself
- when your friend helps you

Things that hinder

- teachers making fun of you in front of the class
- teachers making you feel stupid
- other pupils laughing at you for trying hard
- people mucking about, keeping you off your work
- when the work is too easy
- when you get too many examples of stuff you already know
- when there is a tense atmosphere

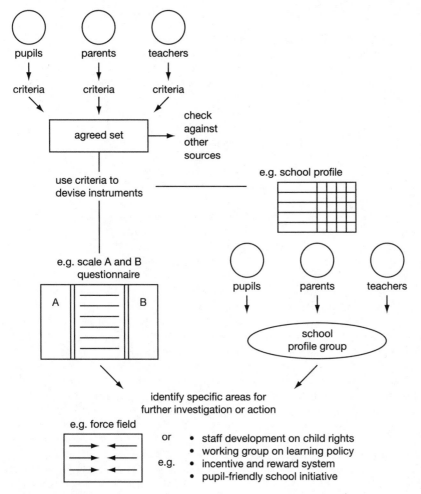

Diagram 10.4 An overview of the process

This can be a whole-school exercise, one carried out at departmental level or it can be used by the individual teacher in his/her own classroom to open discussion, establish groundwork and involve pupils in the ongoing evaluation of learning and teaching. An overview of the process is shown in Diagram 10.4.

11

USING THE FRAMEWORK

In this chapter we have set out the ten clusters and within each five examples of individual indicators. These should be seen as illustrative rather than as comprehensive or exhaustive. For each of the five indicators, we have suggested some sources of evidence that might be gathered, both quantitative and qualitative. These, again, are suggested as illustrative examples only and we would encourage schools to think of their own sources. There is inevitably some repetition but we have assumed that a school undertaking the exercise will proceed in only one or two areas and therefore each cluster is self-contained.

For each set of five indicators, there are corresponding suggestions for a few approaches or instruments that might be relevant to that area of evaluation. Most of these are taken from schools that have used them and found them to be helpful. A few were simply invented and have not, to our knowledge, been tried. A brainstorming workshop with school staff, parents or pupils would generate many more instruments that could be used. Those suggested here might provide a useful starting point for such an exercise.

Most of the approaches suggested would lend themselves to longitudinal use: that is, taking a baseline measure and returning to the same set of questions at regular intervals, say, every six months. They would thus provide 'value-added' information on school or classroom climate, support for teaching or learning, or equity, for example. As part of that process, they might be used for setting targets and measuring gains made against those targets. The beauty of self-evaluation, in our experience, is that once people get the opportunity to be creative and try things out they go well beyond the imagination of their political masters or educational mentors.

1. INDICATOR – SCHOOL CLIMATE

Element	Quantitative evidence	Qualitative evidence	Methods/Instruments
Staff and students behave in a relaxed and orderly way	School rules mentioning specific forms of behaviour/ misbehaviour Incentives/sanctions used at whole-school level Incidence of indiscipline Information for parents	Traffic movement in corridors Atmosphere in lunchrooms State of toilets, policy and supervision of toilets Condition of buildings Roles of staff/students in maintaining order	Content analysis of school rules and values Survey of pupil use of different areas Survey of staff use of different areas Observation schedules for classroom, corridor, playground activity Information to dining-room staff
There are places for pupils to go and constructive things to do outside class time	Numbers of pupils going home at lunchtime Numbers of pupils using school facilities at break times Opportunities for constructive activities in school and playground	Feelings of trust among pupils Atmosphere in study/ social areas Respect shown by pupils for school property Role of support staff in monitoring behaviour/use of facilities	Surveys of parents on school provision e.g. lunches Playground survey of pupil activity Recording of vandalism and graffiti and action taken to remove it
The school is a safe and happy place	Attendance rates: pupils and staff Safety measures taken by school Incidence of bullying, harassment Numbers of staff sending pupils to other schools Placing requests in/out of the school	Perceived attractiveness of the school environment Staff attitudes to pupils and parents Pupil feelings of safety Staff feelings of safety and absence of threat from the local community	Analysis of bullying, harassment of pupils Survey of local parents sending children to other schools Surveys of pupil, parent and staff attitudes
Pupils, staff and parents feel that their contribution to the school is valued	Staff participation in informal school events Membership of PTA Attendance at school meetings and events Pupil membership of clubs, choirs	Willingness of staff to return to school for evening functions or school trips Pupil pride in school and sense of belonging	Walk about/observation schedules Surveys of school users Audit of physical condition of buildings Surveys of parents, staff, pupil attitudes to school
The school is welcoming to visitors and newcomers	Numbers of scheduled and impromptu visits by parents Visits by non-parent members of the community/local industry Use of special provision, e.g. parents' room	Confidence of parents about visiting/ dropping in Nature of language of school notices and posters Opportunities for people to make suggestions and explore alternatives	Entries in visitors' book Suggestion boxes Evaluation forms by supply teachers First-impressions questionnaires for new pupils

SCHOOL CLIMATE

THE FOYER FOLIO

A secondary school has in its foyer a form to be filled out by parents or other visitors to the school while they are waiting for an appointment or on leaving the school. It asks questions such as:

	yes	no	not relevant
I knew where to go	☐	☐	☐
I felt welcome in the school	☐	☐	☐
There were/was clear signposting	☐	☐	☐
Office staff were helpful	☐	☐	☐
Pupils were polite	☐	☐	☐
People said hello or smiled	☐	☐	☐
I was kept waiting without explanation	☐	☐	☐

Write one word to describe your impression on entering the school

_____

Do you have any suggestions as to how we might improve things for parents or other visitors to the school?

INFORMATION ON SUPPLY

A few schools use supply teachers as a source of feedback on the school climate and culture. They are asked to fill this out before they leave. They include questions such as:

- the welcome they received
- nature of information received
- attitudes of pupils
- staffroom ethos
- staff–pupil relationships
- support from staff
- support from management
- comparison with other schools

ETHOS INDICATORS

The Scottish Office Education Department has developed twelve ethos indicators. The following is an activity for Scottish school boards which might well be used or adapted by a board of governors:

Members of the board are asked individually to rate their school on a four-point scale (1 = excellent 4 = lots of room for improvement) with regard to each of the twelve indicators. They then get into groups of three and try to reach agreement as a triad. They then report back to the group as a whole.

The 12 indicators	My rating	Board rating
Pupil morale		
Teacher morale		
Teachers' job satisfaction		
The physical environment		
The learning context		
Teacher–pupil relationships		
Discipline		
Equality and justice		
Extra-curricular activities		
School leadership		
Information to parents		
Parent–teacher consultation		

2. INDICATOR – RELATIONSHIPS

Element	Quantitative evidence	Qualitative evidence	Methods/Instruments
There is a shared sense of teamwork among all staff	Opportunities for joint staff working within the timetable Participation in school committees and working parties Incidence of shared planning/teaching	Staff feel that their views are valued Staff seek out colleagues for support Staff feel ownership of policies Staff value use of INSET Staff offer constructive criticism or advice	Survey of uses of staff time Review of school documentation Staff feedback forms, e.g. evaluation forms after INSET Peer observation/feedback
Older pupils help younger ones	Numbers involved in giving and receiving help Numbers involved in paired schemes, e.g. paired reading Positions of responsibility held by pupils	Younger pupils trust older pupils Pupils see one another as sources of help and support Prefects and senior pupils feel a part of the pupil body	Recording of participation rates Pupil diaries, logs Self-assessment forms Pupil evaluations
Parents and governors feel welcomed and valued in the school	Numbers of parents attending meetings Numbers using school facilities, e.g. drop-in rooms Frequency of newsletters	Parents feel able to come to the school Staff are seen as approachable Parents value parents' evenings Staff feel appreciated by parents	Analysis of numbers of parents visiting school/attending meetings Review of tone/accessibility of school documents Parent questionnaires Exit surveys
Bullying is not tolerated	Incidence of bullying, referrals and actions taken Information to parents Incidence of attendance/school refusal Positive relationships policies	Pupils feel that school is safe Pupils know who to approach for help and advice Parents have confidence in school procedures	Mapping of safe/danger areas Analysis of incidents/referrals Pupil interviews Content analysis of Personal and Social Development programmes Parent interviews
People address one another in ways which confirm their value as individuals	Staff knowledge of pupil names Rules/ground rules in classrooms Opportunities for staff and pupils to discuss outside interests/concerns Differences in name usage by gender race, ability	Pupils and staff feel relaxed with one another in and out of school Names/titles used include rather than exclude individuals Staff feel respected by pupils Pupils feel respected by staff	Numbers attending trips/extra-curricular activities Analysis of policies on names/titles Observation schedules Time sample of words used in classroom/playground

RELATIONSHIPS

OBSERVATION SCHEDULE

A number of the governors are asked to come in for a day each – any day without prior notice. They are to be given as free a run of the school as possible, and access to classrooms has been agreed with staff. An observation schedule has been worked out at the governors' meeting and shared with the staff previously.

The following is only a suggestion of some of the items which might be included:

- What is the attitude of pupils to one another?
- What is the attitude of pupils to teachers?
- What are relations among teachers like?
- Is there a sense of order and purpose in the school?
- Do people care for their environment?
- How were you received as a visitor?
- Do classrooms appear stimulating?
- Do all pupils appear motivated?
- What is your general impression of the ethos of the school?

Clearly, the questions would be tailored to the school and to any strengths and weaknesses perceived.

WHAT'S IN A NAME?

Use of words is an important signal of how seriously people take issues of equity and respect for individuals. A simple way of quantifying this is by keeping a simple checklist of forms of address used by teachers, pupils or others in different contexts over a specific period of time. Pupils might keep their own individual tally of words used to refer to them. We have included a few below suggested by pupils. It might provide a useful starting point for discussion and policy development.

Classes 2.00–3.30	Lunchtime	Playground 10.30–10.40
superstar	the girl in green	uncool
Bill	dozey	rabbit face
boy	luv	the best
sad case	Wilma Smith	Kamal
always the last	cool	mate
Mr Brown	child	Camel
toe-rag		hey you
		Popadom

3. INDICATOR – CLASSROOM CLIMATE

Element	Quantitative evidence	Qualitative evidence	Methods/Instruments
The classroom is a satisfying place to be for pupils and teachers	Displays of work by category pupil and level of achievement Incidence of graffiti/vandalism Pupil attendance and latecoming Staff attendance and latecoming Pupil initiatives in classroom design	Nature/quality and messages conveyed by work displayed Pupil enjoyment and morale Staff enjoyment and morale Parental views of classroom climate Views of support staff on provision	Analysis of attendance Classroom observation Feedback from student teachers Parent /governor surveys on open days Force field analysis (see box)
There is order, purpose and a relaxed atmosphere in classrooms	Referrals for good behaviour Referrals for classroom discipline Time on task Public displays of classroom ground rules or principles Assessment information	Pupil views of classrooms as places where learning can take place Views on consistency of practice across the school Confidence of parents/governors Teacher use of planning time	Analysis of positive and negative referrals Triangulation of different views of classroom climate Regular monitoring of classrooms Grids: focus on classroom interaction
Pupils feel confident in approaching teachers for help	Requests for help/assistance Categories of pupils asking for help (by ability, gender, social class) Uses of learning support Provision for most and least able Approaches to teachers outside class	Role of learning support staff Pupil confidence and ease with staff Nature of informal contacts between pupils and teachers Staff's verbal and non-verbal language	Observation schedules Interviews Pupil logs and diaries Analysis of pupil self-referrals for learning support
Pupils work co-operatively as appropriate	Balance and use of different teaching methodologies Opportunities for pupils to collaborate Range of methodologies in use across the curriculum Policies on peer support/counselling	Teachers' rationale for different learning styles Pupil satisfaction with different learning styles Staff opportunities to observe/work with colleagues in other stages/departments	Sociometric analysis Peer evaluation checklists Analysis of teacher talk/pupil talk Pupil shadowing tracking range of learning/teaching methods used Linking of learning styles to pupil outcomes
No child is excluded from the possibility of success	Analysis of progress by individual and categories of pupil Relative performance ratings by departments/classes Policies on differentiation Progress of pupils with special needs	Pupil sense of belonging/exclusion Staff confidence in the working of the system Parents' satisfaction with child's enjoyment and progress Overview of senior management on coherence/consistency	Analysis of pupil assessment Interviews with pupils, parents, governors, staff Diaries and logs Parent feedback forms Staff review of test and examination results

CLASSROOM CLIMATE

'SMILE, PLEASE!'

One of the classrooms in a school in the study had its set of rules which had been agreed with the pupils. Rule 6 said, 'Wear a Smile'.

If, as pupils say in study after study, they want classrooms to be well ordered, relaxed and places where a sense of humour is present, how can such an atmosphere be created?

One way of getting at answers to this question is to video classroom interaction. It needs:

- volunteers
- a range of teacher styles to be represented
- a professional climate of trust for these to be discussed at staff development sessions

Local teacher education institutions would be only too happy to provide the hardware and the expertise. Failing that, most secondary schools have video equipment, including some editing facilities which can be used.
   Remember *You've Been Framed* pays £250 for every clip used!

THE FORCE FIELD

With some classes where there was time we used a 'force field' analysis to examine some of the pros and cons of support for learning. A form is given to pupils asking them to write on each of the arrows things that helped and things that hindered their learning. The following is one example:

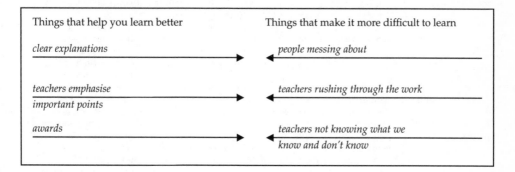

Things that help you learn better	Things that make it more difficult to learn
clear explanations	*people messing about*
teachers emphasise important points	*teachers rushing through the work*
awards	*teachers not knowing what we know and don't know*

SOCIOMETRY

Sociometric analysis is a simple tool that looks at people's relationships with one another. In this context it can be used to look at where and how pupils get support for learning. This technique may be used by an observer or by pupils themselves. In this case the observer has noted in a time segment of fifteen minutes who the child (black dot) went to for help or got help from.

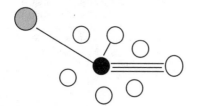

The child herself might use it to plot the three people she gets most help from. People at home (parents, brothers, sisters or grannies) might be included in this. There are many different ways of using this technique.

4. INDICATOR – SUPPORT FOR LEARNING

Indicator	Quantitative evidence	Qualitative evidence	Methods/Instruments
Pupils see themselves as independent learners	Use/take-up of learning support Number of pupils receiving help Pupil use of self-study time Use of library, software and resource materials Balance of teaching/independent learning time	Pupils' view of themselves as learners Views of learning support by staff, pupils, parents and governors Atmosphere in classrooms as work begins Attitudes of pupils to opportunities for self-study	Analysis of learning support use by category/status of pupil Interviews with pupils of varying abilities Logs of pupil use of time Assessment of learning styles
Teachers believe that all pupils can learn and gain success	Rates of progress among various groups of pupils Use of streaming, setting/mixed ability Use of terminology to describe learners–staff, governors, parents	Pupils' aspirations and expectations Staff perception of pupils' aspirations and expectations Range of pupils taking part in study support/extra-curricular activity Attitudes to records of achievement	Surveys of teaching methods Analysis of assessment information Interviews with groups of pupils Logs of pupil experiences Plotting of achievement by social and ethnic background
The main focus of school activity is related to making learning more effective	References to learning in school policies Comparison of rates of progress by different pupil groups Time given to learning and teaching in the school week	Pupil self-esteem Structure of timetable Challenges to labelling by staff Extent to which learning and teaching is discussed informally by staff References to pupil learning in accreditation	Analysis of background factors affecting pupil progress Analysis of timetable and its impact on learning and teaching Pupil and teacher questionnaires Survey of references to learning and teaching in official documents
Learning in and out of school is seen as a coherent whole	Amount, timing and distribution of homework Parental involvement in learning out of school Use of peer learning Incidence of study support schemes	Pupils see school learning as relevant Parents feel part of pupil learning Pupils feel challenged in classrooms Homework is seen as relevant Learning/achievement outside school is recognised and valued	Analysis of homework policy and practice Pupil logs of homework/home study Interviews/questionnaires Uptake by different groups of pupils' study support
Pupils are involved in reviewing progress, recording achievement and target-setting	Assessment and progress data Policies on individual learning, target-setting Use by pupils of target setting Pupil time allocated for completion of records of achievement Staff time allowed for review	Pupils' views of their own progress Value given by pupils to records of achievement Use of records of achievement across the school as a whole Pupil self-confidence and aspirations	Analysis of assessment information Logs of pupil experience Cost-benefit analysis of records of achievement Sampling of profiles across the curriculum and by high/low achievers

SUPPORT FOR LEARNING

THE VOICE OF THE PUPIL

Most teachers welcome feedback from their pupils if it is constructive and is aimed at making support for learning more effective for the class as a whole, or for certain pupils within the class. Periodic evaluation of pupils – based on agreed aims and outcomes – can be a help to teachers in focusing on what they are trying to achieve.

A simple format:

1 Did the lesson/topic achieve its stated purposes?
2 Did you find the work:
   - too easy
   - just about right
   - too difficult
3 Were you able to ask for help if you didn't understand something?
4 Which of the ways of working were most helpful?:
   - individually
   - in pairs
   - in groups
   - as a class
   - with technology (described)

HOMEWORK AND WORK AT HOME

Support for learning is tested most when the pupil is on his/her own, for example, doing homework. How can its usefulness be gauged? The Homework File is a resource pack for schools and governors which supports joint staff development on issues connected with homework. It has a number of purposes and uses. One section of the file is concerned with auditing school/departmental/classroom policy and practice and with evaluating how pupils work at home. The log is kept by a pupil over one week. It can then be used to look at distribution of work at different stages or by different ability groups.

HOMEWORK LOG

Time started	Time finished	Time spent	Subject or kind of homework	Did the teacher give it out or did you decide to do it?	When was it given out?	When has it to be done by?	Difficulties?	Help given?
6.25pm	6.45pm	20mins	Chemistry Problems	Teacher	Today	Tomorrow	Yes!	none
7.00pm	7.45pm	45mins	Maths Questions	Teacher	Today	Tomorrow	Yes	Yes, a friend
11.00pm	11.45pm	45mins	French Read book	Teacher	ongoing		couldn't understand it	None
4.00pm	4.30pm	30mins	(piano) music practice	me (daily practice)	ongoing	no		
4.30pm	5.00pm	30mins	music (violin) practice	me (daily practice)	ongoing	no	—	

Complete the chart by, in the appropriate column, indicating the present position by a tick (✓), and the position you hope to reach by the end of this session by a cross (X).	Not Practice	Under Review	Being Developed	Almost Developed	Current Practice
Homework is closely related to class work.					
Homework tasks involve a variety of activities.					
There is a clear pattern re issuing etc.					
Homework tasks are differentiated.					
All homework is purposeful and useful.					
Pupils are given adequate notice.					
Tasks are issued in written form.					
Teachers keep a homework record.					
Individual homework is monitored.					
Depts are aware of other depts' demands.					
An outline of homework is available.					
Homework is discussed in light of 5–14.					

The questionnaire opposite can be used by schools to survey, or audit, homework policy at departmental level.

The Department hope to achieve the targets indicated (x) by October '99.

Signed: _____ (P.T.)

5. INDICATOR – SUPPORT FOR TEACHING

Element	Quantitative evidence	Qualitative evidence	Methods/Instruments
Support for learning and teaching are at the heart of school policies and planning	References in development plan/policy to classroom practice Assessment data Emphasis on the curriculum in school documents/INSET Success in meeting targets	Staff perceptions of the impact of policies Pupil insight into teaching approaches Governors' confidence in school plans Parental involvement in school's planning process	Review of documentation Interviews/surveys of views of pupils, parents, governors and staff Analysis of development plan targets Shadowing of pupils/classes
Teachers receive effective support from management	Uptake of staff development Use of learning support/timetable Opportunities for career review Opportunities for staff to meet with school management Job remits of management posts	Staff confidence in senior management Teacher sense of developing professionally Priority given by management to staff development	Interviews/questionnaires on support from senior and middle management Diaries of managers/staff Review of stage/departmental plans and targets Evaluation of career review Analysis of minutes of meetings, etc.
The size of classes ensures that all teachers can teach effectively	Review of class sizes by age and stage Comparative rates of progress of groups of pupils Use of learning support Range of teaching methods used	Teacher satisfaction/frustration Pupils' view of access to teachers Support staff views on pupil needs Atmosphere in classrooms Parental confidence that pupils' needs are being met	Analysis of homework marking and time spent on assessment records Recording of individual pupil/staff contact time Survey of traffic flow, logistics, etc. Review of assessment/progress
Teachers share successes and problems with one another	Opportunities for staff to meet and discuss formally and informally Initiatives taken by staff to share and support learning/teaching Uptake of in-service opportunities Management initiatives in place	Staff valuing of formal and informal opportunities for support Use of INSET time Use of timetabled meetings	Review of systems for staff support Review of documentation Incidence of co-operative teaching Peer observation Teacher diaries
Parents are seen as partners in the pupils' learning	Information on curriculum/methods Parental uptake of meetings on curriculum/teaching and learning Opportunities for parents to comment and share views on pupils' learning Parental monitoring/comments on homework	Language and tone of parental communications Parental knowledge and interest in pupils' learning Nature of parents' comments on homework	Review of parental contacts Home–school diaries Parent surveys/interviews Governors sample pupil reports, looking at pupil/staff/parental comments

SUPPORT FOR TEACHING

CLASS SIZE – SECONDARY

Class size came up in a number of schools visited in this study. There was clearly a perception that classes were too big but the issue tended to be discussed in the absence of any information or supporting evidence.

In secondary schools staff are often only aware of the size of their own class and may only have an impression of the situation in other classes.

What factors influence class size?

In a secondary school a member of staff volunteered to conduct a survey an present the findings back to staff, governors and parents.

For example:

1   What is the staffing complement and how is it arrived at?
2   What is the distribution of staff and why?
3   How many pupils are there? Are projected?
4   What courses/classes must run (NC: pupils already made choices, etc.)
5   What timetabling constraints are there (accommodation, subject specialisms, college links, etc.)
6   What school policies impinge on the timetable (co-operative teaching, PSD, etc.)
7   What leeway is there in the timetable for raising or lowering class size?

PARENTAL SUPPORT

A half-page in the Pupil Report is given over for parents to comment on their support for their children's learning at home and in school. How many do respond and what do they say?

Feed these back in a collated form to staff for discussion

Invite in a group of parents to discuss some of the (anonymised) comments and their implications.

QUALITY TIME

Teachers are asked over a school term/session to keep a log of their non-class contact time:

* preparation
* meetings
* INSET
* marking
* extra-curricular, etc.

They are asked to rate on a 1–5 scale:

* extremely useful
* useful
* neutral
* not very useful
* waste of time

how they felt the activity had added to their effectiveness as teachers.

A pro forma for the activity might be drawn up. In addition, if they have time, they are asked to make any comments on what would have improved the activity.

The returns are made to a small committee of staff who produce a collated report for discussion at a staff development session.

6. INDICATOR – TIME AND RESOURCES

Element	Quantitative evidence	Qualitative evidence	Methods/Instruments
Organisation of classes is conducive to all pupils learning effectively	Numbers in classes by stage/subject/year group Uses of grouping/withdrawal Range of teaching methods used Indiscipline rates/achievement Assessment of progress Incidence of co-operative teaching	Staff views of principles of organisation Pupil views of learning and teaching approaches Parental perceptions of their children's progress Governors' understanding of issues	Breakdown of assessment/examination results by class Surveys of methodologies in use Interviews/surveys on use of learning support/special provision Shadowing classes
Deployment of resources is the result of a shared negotiated approach	Budgeting and allocations of resources Dissemination of relevant information to staff, governors, parents Involvement of individuals in decision-making Costs–benefits analysis	Staff confidence in decision-making Staff feelings of inclusion Staff sense of fairness Awareness of procedures among staff Information and understanding of governors of resource issues	Analysis of records/minutes of meetings Numbers of staff involved in various activities Review of staff use of resources Review of pupil use of resources Survey of governor views
Time for teachers to plan, assess and develop professionally is well used	Time usage across the school Time usage by staff outside school Uptake of staff development Bids for development time Opportunities for staff to meet formally and informally	Staff sense of their own expertise Feelings of confidence in, and support from, school management Value placed on meetings by staff Staff views on usefulness of formal and informal meetings	Analysis of time/uptake levels among teachers of INSET Staff surveys of use of development time Review of spending on staff development
Resources are available to pupils within and outwith the school day	Availability of resources to pupils Rates of usage of school resources Damage/misuse of equipment Provision of opportunities before and after school, e.g. study support, breakfast clubs	Pupil satisfaction with provision and access to resources Valuing by parents of opportunities for use of school resources Pupils' view of opportunities offered Perceived need for after-school clubs	Statistical breakdown by age of groups using facilities Surveys of staff and pupils Analysis of staff needs Attendance patterns at homework clubs/study support
The school is a community resource	Usage of school by outside agencies Range of activities on offer Recording of outcomes and achievements by community users Recording of any problems/issues Monitoring of visits to the school	View of external organisation Views of staff and pupils within the school Esteem of the school in the local area Accessibility of the school Expectations of the school	Analysis of uptake of out-of-school activities Interviews with users User surveys Documentation: the impact on users Case studies of innovative use

TIME AND RESOURCES

SUBJECT_____   PERIOD_____

Minutes into lesson	5	10	15	20	25	30	35	40	45	50	55	60	65	70	75	80
Nature of pupil activity																
Pupil working																
• on own																
• in pairs																
• in a group																
Pupil																
• Speaking																
• listening																
• viewing																
• writing, note-taking																
extended																
short answer																
• reading																
• practical																
Nature of teacher activity																
Teacher exposition or demonstration with no interaction																
Teacher interaction with																
• individual pupil																
• pair of pupils																
• group of pupils																
• whole class																
Nature of materials in use																
• textbook																
• school produced booklet																
• work guide																
• work sheet																
Technological side																
• video																
• audio																
• computer																
• slides																
• word processor																
• calculator																
• spellmaster																

CLASSROOM OBSERVATION SCHEDULE

A secondary school is concerned about the relationship between use of resources, time and the range of teaching methods employed across the curriculum. How was time used? To what extent was learning differentiated? Were methods appropriate?

The school asked for volunteers across the staff to become part of a 'pupil shadowing' team. The team was given time to work with an external, 'critical friend' to decide on what it is they were looking for, how they would carry out the task, how they would handle 'ethical' issues such as confidentiality and how they could remain objective and non-judgemental. After a period of time, they arrive at the schedule (opposite)

Time was created for each of the team of eight teachers to shadow a class for a day. (The time is 'bought' from the absence cover budget.) After the operation is complete, the 'critical friend' meets the group and there is a debriefing and analysis of what is found.

DIARIES

Getting people to keep a diary for a specific period of time is a technique used by researchers, often with very interesting results. One method used recently with a sample of Scottish and English headteachers was to get them to keep a diary of what they did over the course of a day from getting up to going to bed. These were then analysed to identify what they did, whom they spoke to, where they went. It gave a picture of how they spent their time and what their priorities were, and headteachers were able to place what they actually did alongside what they said was important as managers. This helped them to see where the discrepancies lay. The exercise could be used by anyone in the school: teachers, support staff, pupils or governors.

SURVEY OF USAGE

Pupils are concerned that they don't get enough access to the school's resources. With the support of the head and staff, some of the senior pupils in the school carry out over a one-month period the rates of usage of different areas, for example:

- library
- computer (room)
- music rooms
- gymnasium

These are broken down by:

- age/stage
- gender
- other categories

Comments are gathered from the users by means of a short questionnaire.

Damage and graffitti are assessed at the outset and again at the end of the period in question.

7. INDICATOR – ORGANISATION AND COMMUNICATION

Element	Quantitative evidence	Qualitative evidence	Methods/Instruments
School decision-making is an open participatory process	Number and status of staff on committees and working parties Opportunities for staff involvement in decision-making Opportunities for staff to make suggestions	Staff confidence in decision-making Atmosphere in meetings Openness of discussion Willingness of staff to join working groups	Analysis of school calendar Process analysis of meetings (see box) Analysis of minutes of governors' meetings Time spent per item (see box)
The views of all within the school are listened to	Opportunities and forums for discussion Number of staff speaking at meetings Rates of return from staff surveys Numbers of parents/governors involved in school committees	Trust and confidence of staff in their colleagues Willingness of staff to share their interests and concerns Handling of disagreements and conflict	Review of people involved in consultation by group/status Audio/video recordings at meetings Review of minutes of meetings and actions taken as a result
Pupils have forums for discussing their concerns and problems	Existence of pupil forums Rates of pupil participation Number of meetings held Evidence of links and feedback between pupil forum and staff Counselling self-referral by pupils	Quality of discussions in pupils' forums Confidence of pupils that staff will listen to their views/concerns Willingness to discuss 'sensitive' items	Surveys of pupil views and expectations Observation of meetings Pupil evaluation of effectiveness Discourse analysis (see box) Triangulation of views (see box)
Parents and governors are informed about school policies and practice	Frequency of parental newsletters/survey returns Governor attendance at, involvement in, information evenings Range of opportunities for discussion among staff/parents/governors	Parental familiarity with school policy Handling of parental complaints Perceived priority given to informing parents Weight given to governors' views	Breakdown of parent returns, e.g. by geographical location, by ability of child Analysis of parental contacts Analysis of governors' attendance at school events by type/group
The community has a strong positive view of the school	Opportunities taken to inform the community of school events Number of mentions of school activities in local press Initiatives taken/funds raised by the community to support the school	Nature of participation of local community in school efforts/events School support for community concerns and events Reputation of the school among local people and business, e.g. shopkeepers	Review of fund-raising trends Content analysis of press coverage Analysis of room to use by school Documenting contacts/initiatives between school and media Surveys of community views

ORGANISATION AND COMMUNICATION

THE LEAFLET DROP

A primary school in a built-up residential area is very conscious of the potential for friction with local residents as children arrive in the morning, go to the local shops at lunchtime and go home at 3.45. The school has had an 'image problem' in the past and has been working hard on ethos, on positive behaviour strategies and on relations with the community. It decides to carry out a leaflet drop to all the local residents, shop-owners and community groups. Pupils design the leaflet which describes the school, its aims and some of what they consider to be its strengths. There is a tear-off slip for suggestions and comments. The drop itself is organised by the senior classes and supervised by staff and parent volunteers.

TELEPHONE SURVEYS

A common set of issues is covered, though the tone of the conversation is informal:

SMT member introduces self, explains the purpose of the call (to reassure in case the parent is alarmed!) and asks if it is convenient to speak for a few minutes:

The key questions are then asked:

- Are the newsletters arriving home?
- Is the style/tone/content OK?
- Is the parent happy with the school report?
- Are parents' evenings satisfactory?
- Is parent happy with progress of child(ren)?
- Could the school do more to involve parents?

In one secondary school each member of the senior management, each term, is allocated a representative group of parents to contact by telephone. The aim of the exercise is to inquire how well the school is communicating with the parents, and how happy parents are with the progress of their child(ren).

VIDEOING MEETINGS

A school is concerned that groups of staff working on development planning are not as productive as they could be. There are vague concerns about lack of training for chairpersons, lack of opportunity for more diffident or less experienced members of staff to contribute. A suggestion is made that the next round of meetings should be recorded on video using a fly-on-the-wall approach. Each group would watch and analyse the videos on the next training day. An external adviser was invited to focus discussion and suggest improvements.

CRITICAL INCIDENT ANALYSIS

One way of getting rich information on the school as an organisation is to test how it handles problems, crises or conflicts. It can be done with a single individual as an interview or with a group (e.g. a group of teachers or a mixed parent–teacher group).

The individual or group identifies an incident in the life of the school that was difficult to handle or created conflict. It might be, for example, a reorganisation, a pupil protest, a disciplinary incident. The group then (preferably with the help of an outsider or critical friend) tries to reconstruct the situation from their own experience, avoiding blame but analysing:

- What happened? Who was involved?
- How effective was action taken?
- What options were available at the time?
- What knowledge at the time would have enabled people to do things differently?
- What might have been done differently?

The same technique can be used to examine the handling of change, or to analyse something that people felt had been a success, identifying the salient strengths of the school.

8. INDICATOR – EQUITY

Element	Quantitative evidence	Qualitative evidence	Methods/Instruments
Pupils have faith in the policy of equal opportunities	Level of involvement of pupils in decision-making Documentation/minutes, etc. Information for pupils on school policy Use of time in pupil councils	Priority given to equal opportunity policy by staff/pupils Perception that the school operates a fair system in all areas Recognition of the need to target positively certain pupils	Review of policy documents Review of steps taken to involve pupils Interviews with samples of pupils Recording of decisions taken in pupil councils and actions taken as a result
Cultural, moral, intellectual and social diversity is seen as adding value to school life and learning	Statistics on pupil uptake of subjects by category Statistics on discipline/attendance Assessment/examination information Information on pupils asking for support	General sense of fairness and justice Staff perceptions of pupil well-being Parental confidence in how children are treated Pupil confidence in support of staff Positive action for minority groups	Statistical breakdowns of curricular choice Logs/shadowing/observation – targeted on groups of pupils for specific issues Targeted observations
All staff believe they have a part to play in promoting an equal opportunity culture	Involvement in staff committees, extra-curricular activities Staff initiatives in school improvement Opportunities for staff to volunteer for service on committees	Staff perceptions of their role Staff 'feel-good factor' Recognition given to staff efforts and contribution by governors and parents Pupils' valuing of initiatives taken by staff	Analysis of staff involvement Analysis of the range of opportunities for staff development Surveys of staff morale/satisfaction Reviews of staff contributions at governor meetings
The planning and organisation of the curriculum takes account of the needs of all children	Incidence of grouping/setting, etc. Use of learning support Assessment and examination by category of pupil Indiscipline/exclusion Post-school destinations of pupils	Staff views of the curriculum Views of timetabling priorities and distribution Pupil perceptions of subjects/topics Atmosphere in classrooms Governors' views on the curriculum	Analysis of curricular planning and timetabling process Observation/shadowing of pupils/classes Analysis of practice in classrooms Analysis of pupil destinations
All pupils have a chance to take responsibility in class, school and extra-curricular activities	Numbers of pupils asking for help Numbers of pupils involved in paired reading, etc. Attendance rates at extra-curricular activities Incidence of pupil mentoring	Pupil perceptions of their status Use of learning support staff Involvement of staff, pupils and others in forums for decision-making Parents and governors involved in promoting pupil participation	Observation/shadowing of pupils Analysis by categories of pupils involved in various activities Logs and diaries Surveys of pupils not involved in extra-curricular activities

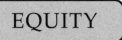

EQUITY

SEMIOTICS

Semiotics is the analysis of hidden messages in pictures and images. In an equal opportunities context the images on school walls and in textbooks are seen as particularly important because they can include or exclude groups or suggest different models of behaviour. They can educate by challenging stereotypes. Many different kinds of checklist have been suggested for this kind of analysis. Most emphasise things such as how many:

- men and how many women?
- different racial groups?
- disabled people?
- men, doing non-traditional 'men jobs'?
- women, doing non-traditional 'women jobs'?
- high-status men? women? disabled people?

INTERPRETING THE EVIDENCE

A school equal opportunities group is looking at a range of issues, from pupil uptake of subjects at GCSE and then at A level by gender; numbers of pupils from areas of disadvantage succeeding in examinations; ethnic variations in participation in school activities. An issue which surfaces is the apparent lack of women in the school showing interest in career progression. Is there an issue of equity here?

The group produces the sheet below for a staff training day. Staff in mixed groups discuss some of the possible explanations offered and suggest at least one other which may be relevant. At the end of the discussion, each group suggests one step the school could take to address any of the issues which have emerged.

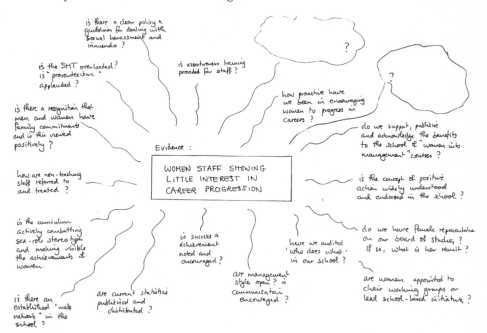

9. INDICATOR – RECOGNITION OF ACHIEVEMENT

Element	Quantitative evidence	Qualitative evidence	Methods/Instruments
There is a climate of achievement in the school	Documentation of achievement by individuals, groups, cohorts Procedures for monitoring progress/ added value Records of achievement Attendance records	Values placed on different kinds of achievement by different groups Quality of pupils' work Community views of school Benefits/drawbacks of systems of monitoring achievement	Analysis of achievement by teachers/departments Sampling analysis of pupil work Review of records of achievement Examination of documentation Surveys of opinions
All pupils have an equal chance of having their achievements recognised	Opportunities for different achievements Support systems for underachieving pupils Achievement by groups in different areas of school/classroom activity	Value placed by teachers on personal achievement and examination success Pupils' identification with school Pupils' sense of being valued Pupils' belief in opportunities to succeed	Breakdown of results/ prizes/extra-curricular activities Review of subject choice Analysis of prize winners by social class, gender, etc. Pupil shadowing
Awards rather than punishment is the prevailing approach throughout the school	Use of praise by teachers Discipline/referral/ exclusion rates Sponsorship of awards schemes Involvement of staff, parents, pupils in development of policies Categories of pupils receiving awards	Atmosphere in the school Values of awards as seen by pupils Pupil self-esteem and target-setting Parents' knowledge of, and support for, school policies Support from outside bodies	Observation schedules Review of newsletters, bulletins, etc. Analysis of use of sanctions by category Parent interviews Employer surveys
There is consensus in the school about what is regarded as success	Involvement of staff, pupils and parents in developing policies Staff use of assessment information Opportunities for staff to monitor and discuss achievement data Extra-curricular involvement of staff	Value placed on choices and opportunities open to pupils Level of agreement about definitions of 'success' Parental attitudes to curriculum subjects and school activities	Consideration of uptake of different courses/activities Uptake of extra-curricular activities by group/ gender/race/age Analysis of governors' minutes Triangulation of survey data
Staff achievements are recognised and rewarded	References to staff in newsletters, press releases, etc. Staff attendance rates Promotions from within the staff Staff volunteering to do extra work Frequency of praise for staff	Value attached to staff for 'praise' and sources of praise Staff knowledge and appreciation of colleagues' work Value given by staff to appraisal Job satisfaction/self-esteem of staff	Peer observation Case studies of good practice Critical incident analysis Analysis of school documentation/minutes Staff survey

RECOGNITION OF ACHIEVEMENT

SAMPLING WORK

The quality of the work produced by young people is the best indicator of learning, progress and added value. One way of doing this that is not too time consuming is to take:

- a random sample of young people
- a random sample of their work at regular intervals

Analysing the quality of that work against a few key criteria may be carried out by a small group of teachers. One primary school where this is done has found it a very productive exercise in giving both a measure of pupil achievement and helping to focus on areas for development.

PLOTTING AND PLANNING

A secondary school head on arriving at school was concerned to look at issues of achievement and recognition. One of the first things she did was to take a map of the area and plot on the map the place where the following came from:

- prize winners
- those who took part in extra-curricular activities
- those who had been excluded

A 'Celebrating Achievement' working group was established to look at the evidence and to consider whether the school was doing enough to:

- recognise achievement across the board
- reward success equally in all fields
- make a link between interests in and out of school
- address the negative aspects of peer pressure
- ensure that social factors were not preventing some students from gaining success and/or participating in school activities

LOGGING THE PRAISE

Ask a range of people within the school – pupils, teachers, support staff, cleaners, cafeteria staff, etc. – to log over a period of time when they receive praise and in what circumstances.

MENTORING

A secondary school developed the following way of tracking individual achievement. Teachers were given the role of mentors with responsibility for three students each. On specific occasions agreed with the classroom teacher they would sit in on the class and observe for a period. Their observation would focus on the three students for whom they had responsibility, assessing the learning that was taking place, not the teaching. They were able to make a number of quantitative and qualitative judgements fed back to, and discussed with, the teacher at the end of the lesson.

- How was the student's time spent?
- How much of it was on task? How much wasted?
- What was she doing? What was her learning style?
- How much help did she get? How much did she need?
- What was she learning? What was the quality of the learning?
- Was she being involved? challenged? making progress?

The lesson learned by teachers was that there was a significant gap between teaching and learning. One concluded: 'There are some really excellent teachers in this school but there are children in their classes who aren't learning.'

WALKING THE TALK

A head of a large secondary school believes strongly in talking with all staff, teaching and support, at least once every week.

To ensure that she does it, she keeps a list of names and ticks off each member of staff as she talks to them. Towards the end of the week she targets those staff whom she has not spoken to that week.

- Is this too mechanistic?
- Would the staff object to such a device if they knew?
- Is it simply an *aide-memoire*?
- Is such human contact important?
- Could others within the school adopt a similar approach?
- Would it work with pupils?

10. INDICATOR – HOME–SCHOOL LINKS

Element	Quantitative evidence	Qualitative evidence	Methods/Instruments
Parents play an active part in their children's learning	Numbers of parents involved in home–school initiatives/workshops Communications from parents about home learning/homework/study Contacts with home/home visiting Availability of parents' rooms	School understanding of the significance of home learning Usefulness of information to parents Staff support/guidance for parents Parental knowledge of curriculum Parents know how to help at home	Examination of records of visits, etc. Home–school diary Uptake of programmes/information Review of documentation/language Surveys and interviews Home–school video
Parents are confident that problems will be dealt with and feedback given	Circulation of school policies Information on, involvement in, policy development Records of complaints/actions taken Logs of telephone, correspondence, visits	School's understanding of the diversity of the parental group Parental awareness of school procedures Attitudes of staff to parental complaints	Analysis of records and logs Analysis of parent contacts by category Case studies/tracking communications Questionnaires for parents
The school provides for the social, cultural and linguistic backgrounds of pupils	Provisions for cultural differences (e.g. timing of meetings) Categories of parents visiting school Provision for pupils (e.g. study support) School use of community languages	Quality of images and diversity of displays around school Parents' feelings of being welcomed Pupil feelings of safety Respect for individuality of pupils and parents	Semiotic analysis (analysis of imagery and hidden messages) Review of uptake of opportunities Community surveys Breakdown of involvement by different community groups
Parent–teacher meetings are useful and productive	Uptake of planned/crises meetings Parents know purpose and agenda for meetings Time spent with teachers Pupils accompanying parents Alternative times for parents to visit	Effectiveness of meetings Context of meetings Atmosphere at meetings Agreed outcomes of meetings Parental sense of being welcome Parental satisfaction with outcomes	Exit surveys Analysis of attendance records by categories Interviews with parents Force field analysis
Pupil progress is monitored and shared with parents on a regular basis	Range of practices for keeping parents informed Frequency of reporting – formal and informal Opportunities for parents to contribute to progress review Language used in reporting	Consistency of practice across a school/department Nature of support for pupils in recording achievements Use made by parents of monitoring procedures Tone of reports/use of language	Review of reports Analysis of reading levels Survey of teachers' time spent in report writing Analysis of parental responses on report forms

HOME–SCHOOL LINKS

TWO-WAY VIDEO

In a special school they use a video record for assessing pupils' progress over time and for keeping a live two-way communication between home and school. The classroom teacher (or anyone who can use a camera) records a short number of sequences of the child engaged in some task. This is then sent home to the parent who can use it for a number of purposes – as a focus for discussion with the child, or with other people in the household, or with teachers. It also provides a value-added record over time. Some parents reciprocate by recording the child's learning at home and send it back to school.

It is not a costly method either in terms of resources or time. Parents can supply the tapes and the recording can be done by anyone in the class, for example, by pupils working in pairs. For them it can be a useful self-evaluation approach too.

REVIEW OF DOCUMENTATION

A small group of governors, parents, teachers and pupils reviews some of the school's external documentation:

- handbook/prospectus
- newsletters
- subject choice booklets

- advice to parents on homework/ support for learning

The group looks at:

- readability
- tone

- layout/format
- suitability for purpose/audience, etc.

and makes recommendations for improvement.

CASE STUDY

To get a true picture of how communication actually works between home and school a few in-depth case studies can be useful. A small sample of pupils may be chosen at random, or selectively to represent different kinds of home backgrounds (large family, lone-parent family, frequent visitor to school, parent unknown to school) and communication traced through to find out what happens at various stages:

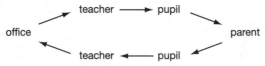

If this is done retrospectively it involves the following steps:

- identify specific pupils (say, five or six)
- identify a recent communication (e.g. newsletter)
- briefly interview office people who play a part in the process, explaining purpose of the exercise
- interview parent(s) – either phone or face-to-face in a little more depth asking for permission and carefully explaining the purpose of the exercise as trying to improve school procedures.
- collate and briefly write up anonymous case studies with recommendations

---

EXIT SURVEY

A school is concerned that the quality of the interaction between parent and teacher at parents' evenings may not be all that it should be. Staff are very conscientious and try hard to ensure that the limited amount of time available is used productively, but they are unsure about the value of this for parents.

Forms are provided for parents to fill in while they are waiting and they are asked to post them in the box provided before they leave. Questions cover:

- Parent waiting time
- Time with teacher(s)
- Attitudes of teacher(s)

- Satisfaction with the outcome
- Suggested improvements

12

SUMMARY AND
RECOMMENDATIONS

The 'Schools Speak for Themselves' study raised some fundamental issues for the research team, for the schools involved, for authorities and for wider policy-making. They are questions which should be at the forefront of thinking and in the public debate.

- What are schools for and who are they for?
- What counts as important and what makes for improvement?
- How should success and improvement be measured?

How we answer these has a number of far-reaching implications for policy at the level of school, local authority and government.

What are schools for and who are they for?

There was a consensus among all groups that schools were primarily places for learning. Most people saw that in terms of pupil learning but some had a wider definition in which 'learners' encompassed a range of possibilities for recurrent and lifelong education and was relevant to the community at large. Learning itself was also defined broadly and was generally expressed as learning for life, for work, for leisure and for personal development.

Support for the personal and social development of young people was similarly emphasised by all groups in this study. Schools were not seen simply as places where cohorts of pupils moved through with a maximum of efficiency. They were seen as social places in which children and young people spent much of their growing-up time, where they developed relationships, some of which would last through their lifetimes. Schools could be an important source of support for parents, not only in terms of their children's learning but at times because they were the only places parents could turn to in a crisis. They sometimes spoke of their debt to teachers for helping them through a difficult period or for putting them in touch with other social agencies which could help them.

Schools were also seen as places for teachers. They were places in which teachers learned how to teach and were enabled to give of themselves to children to the degree that they themselves had opportunities to develop satisfying relationships and opportunities to learn. Teachers could be seen, in a sense, as 'internal clients' of the school in that their needs had to be met for the school to be productive or effective. They may also be seen as the single most important investment which a government can make in the future. A critical measure of school improvement is the capacity of teachers to be leaders and shapers of education in the next millennium.

What counts as success?

Successful schools are successful for people in a range of different ways. They can be measured by the quality of experience they offer to young people, their ability to support and challenge and 'bring out the best in them'. Bringing out the best was what good teachers did. Pupils' experience of 'school' was important but the seminal influences on their development were through the influence of good teachers. In pupils' repertoires of indicators 'support for learning' was their most significant category and it referred overwhelmingly to the skills and qualities of their teachers.

School effectiveness research reminds us that a good school is more than a collection of good teachers, but it also strongly supports the argument that the 'teacher effect' is the one we should pay most attention to.

Successful pupils were those who not only gained qualifications but became more responsible, confident, inventive and enterprising. They played a part in school life and contributed to their school and their classmates. Some tutored and counselled their peers and younger children, informally and as a formal aspect of the school organisation. Some pupils played a part in making the school a better place for those who followed. They had a school improvement role too.

If success at individual and school level is to be assured it follows that everyone in the school community carries some form of responsibility and accountability. That is most likely to be realised in practice if people's expectations of one another are understood and if there is a climate in the school which is receptive to critical review and improvement at all levels.

If success is defined broadly and developmentally it does not seem appropriate to place all the emphasis on narrow partial measures of attainment. Good schools are a rich mix and not easily reduced to a set of statistics. Examination success is the right of every pupil and they should not be sold short, but nor should their quality of school life be narrowed and distorted in some of the ways that were described to us by pupils and teachers in this study.

Value-added is widely seen as a fairer way of evaluating schools because it takes into account the baseline from which pupils and schools start. 'Controlling for the quality of intake' is a phrase that has been used by researchers in pursuit of a value-added model,[1] but if 'quality' refers simply to specific measures of prior attainment, it is a serious distortion of the term. It leads us down the dangerous path of schools selecting pupils who carry with them variable price tags. It is, in the words of one governor, not just about bums on seats but 'quality bums' on seats.

A better model of value-added can be seen in the special school context where it means charting growth in individual and collective terms, celebrating achievements that for some might be totally insignificant but for others are giant steps. The concept of value-added makes most sense when it is grounded in the real world of what matters to pupils, parents and teachers. The main message emerging from this study is that those who live day to day in classrooms and schools should play a major role in evaluating their experiences, their successes and priorities for future development. This cannot be divorced from external evaluation and the role played by local and national inspection. Most researchers agree that a robust system of evaluation needs both internal and external sources.[2] However, the respective roles of each should be clearly understood and allocated accordingly.

Self-evaluation has its strongest appeal in healthy dynamic schools with a keen interest in improvement. Its attractions are likely to be least in schools which lack self-confidence and would rather deny than expose their weaknesses. There is a continuum of outside support that is needed, with very little or none at one end to strong and sustained support and intervention at the other. Self-confident schools can be brash, adventurous and even foolhardy in their risk-taking but vulnerable schools need to be more cautious and pragmatic, and above all they need a sense of self-belief and competence which has to come from an outside critical friend. Some schools may be seen as suffering from learning difficulties. These could be as acute in high-achieving complacent schools as in low-achieving embattled schools. Resistance to learning and change may be just as profound and deep-seated in the high-attaining schools as in embattled schools. Their status in performance tables and inundation with placing requests from other areas can serve to mask the differentials of achievement, uncritical attitudes to learning among teachers and pupils, and a divisive 'balkanised' school culture.

The balance of internal and external evaluation needs to be weighed in respect of each individual school but in every school some element of self-evaluation has to be present because it is the seed of growth. In vulnerable, struggling schools self-evaluation may have to start small and be limited to those areas where the school feels there is something to build on. On the other hand, the nature of its problems may be so self-evident that it is willing, with support and help from the outside, to focus from the start on areas of salient weakness. Complacent and self-satisfied schools may also need considerable support to deal with the dissonance between the way things are and the way they would like to believe they are.

It is also a matter of how we define 'the school'. Failing schools are often, as we know from both research and day-to-day experience, a reflection of ineffective headteachers. Teachers in such schools are, in our experience, often enthusiastic about self-evaluation precisely because they hope to expose the problems at headteacher or senior management level. Nor are many, if any, schools ineffective through and through. Most schools are curate's eggs, almost always with good parts, and with good teachers who are often failing to thrive because they are in a stifling climate. There are teachers often carrying disproportionate burdens of responsibility because of ineffective management, or being given no adequate support by the headteacher, local authority or national government.

A system of evaluation designed to support and challenge schools should, as with sound learning theory, start from individual needs and prior learning. An upward system of accountability would examine layer by layer from the bottom up what is needed to support effectiveness and improvement. The top tier of school inspection and review should concern itself with how the different layers of the system are accountable to the classroom teacher, and ultimately to the child, for the climate which they help to create for successful learning.

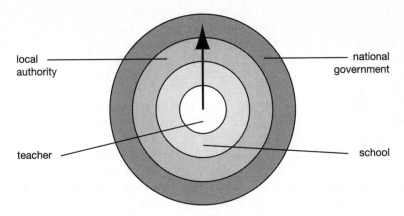

Diagram 12.1 Accountability – support for learning and teaching

An integrated system

There does not yet exist in England and Wales a system which brings internal and external school evaluation together in a coherent and systematic way, drawing on the strengths of both and conceptualising quality assurance as an integrated system of support for learning and teaching. There are interesting developments in other countries which should be examined closely, at least in terms of some of their guiding principles. The following are some such principles:

- the conduct and focus of the external review is discussed and negotiated with the school
- criteria used in external evaluation are disseminated, discussed and made meaningful to those to whom they apply
- there is a protocol of behaviour, interpersonal relationships and professional respect which is understood and agreed
- the school has faith in the competence and credibility of the review team
- the review team contains a mixture of people, some who are familiar with the school and some who come with no prior knowledge
- review teams are accountable to schools for the quality of their work
- the process is seen by the key stakeholders as worthwhile and as supporting school and classroom development
- responsibilities for evaluation are shared between external and internal sources as appropriate
- the focus of the external review is primarily on quality of the school's own approach to self-improvement and with its capacity for change
- the review team takes time to get to know the school and its community before embarking on a review or inspection

The opportunity for a review team to spend time in the local community talking to people and gauging their expectations (as is done in British Columbia) is a useful prelude to school visits. The Australian practice of composing the review team of 50 per cent insiders and 50 per cent outsiders may also be a way of achieving the right balance. We also think it is vital that the school's and the community's own criteria be discussed along with the agenda brought by the outside review team. We do not think it is helpful to come with a set of generalised criteria drawn from best practice elsewhere and expect schools to accept these as valid or achievable targets.

Drawing on Stephen Ball's work, we conclude that quality assurance and school improvement is everybody's business.[3] It is a developmental system in which people have ownership of and take pride in the quality of their work and where systems are put into place to support that. Teachers should not be expected to shoulder the burden of accountability just as individual schools should not be expected to be self-sufficient in a competitive market. There have to be systems of support at every level, from the classroom to the local authority. Quality assurance is collegial rather than hierarchical and about prevention from the inside rather than 'cure' from the outside. It cannot work in a climate of threat and sanctions, nor can it be sustained in a climate where teachers and schools compete to achieve goals which they do not believe in.

RECOMMENDATIONS

The commitment by the government to 'education, education, education' is welcome, and timely. It has a key role to play in informing and stimulating a wider public debate on school success and successful schools. This must involve a reappraisal of the ways in which school achievement is evaluated and reported nationally. This should be undertaken in the light of experience in other countries. Following best practice elsewhere, priority should be given to developing a collaborative model of school evaluation, one which gives greater responsibility and control to individual schools and to classroom teachers.

The model of beacon schools can be adapted to support learning exchange networks, accompanied by an appropriate level of funding, helping to draw together and to disseminate principles of good practice in school self-evaluation and improvement planning. Opportunities ought to exist for teachers to engage in critical discussion of school evaluation criteria and tools of measurement in a way that supports rather than detracts from learning and teaching. Governors too have an important role to play and can, with support and training opportunities, contribute significantly to evaluation and improvement. Information to parents should offer them ways of understanding and evaluating schools and they should have honest practical advice about what part they can play in the process.

Local authorities have a critical part to play in supporting and sustaining an evaluation culture at school and classroom level and should be integrally involved in that process. Researchers could do more work with authorities and schools, helping to develop ways of adapting evaluation strategies and techniques to make them accessible, economical and user friendly for schools and teachers. Researchers might also be persuaded, through funding mechanisms and reappraisal of what counts as 'good research', to give a higher priority to making findings of research accessible to teachers, governors, parents and school students.

It should be recognised that the effectiveness of teachers hinges on an optimum amount of time, level of resourcing and class size. It has also to be acknowledged that effective school evaluation and improvement, like effective teaching, can only take place where there is teacher goodwill and high teacher morale. A realistic calculation of costs (including stress-related illness and absenteeism) in relation to priorities should be made to identify ways in which teacher time and resources could be used more effectively.

FOUR KEY PRIORITIES

- Self-evaluation should be central in any national approach to school improvement.
- Accountability and self-improvement should be seen as two strands of a single interrelated strategy.
- Provision of time and resources has to feature as a key issue in school improvement.
- School inspection should continue to be a feature of the drive towards school improvement, but as part of a collaborative strategy with schools and local authorities.

NOTES

1 WHY SCHOOLS MUST SPEAK FOR THEMSELVES

1 Frost, R. (1995) *Improvement through Inspection*, National Commission of Education Briefing no. 9.
2 Coleman, P. and Collinge, J. (1995) 'An inside-out approach to school improvement', paper delivered at Eighth Annual Congress for School Effectiveness and School Improvement, Leeuwarden, January.
3 The approach adopted in Chicago schools is discussed in greater detail in James Learmonth's case study that appears in Chapter 8 of this book.
4 Schratz, M. and Steiner-Löffler, U. (1998) *Die Lemende Schule*, Weinheim, Beltz Verlag.
5 Fullan, M.G. (1991) *The New Meaning of Educational Change*, New York, Teachers' College Press.
6 House, E. (1973) *School Evaluation: The Politics and Process*, San Francisco, McCutchan Publishing Corporation.
7 Gray, J. and Wilcox, B. (1995) *Good School. Bad School: Evaluating Performance and Encouraging Improvement*, Milton Keynes, Open University Press, p. 16.
8 Ibid., p. 41.
9 Hoyle, E. (1975) 'The Study of Schools as Organisations', in V. Houghton, R. McHugh and C. Morgan (eds) *Management in Education: Reader 1*, London, Ward Lock.
10 Hewton, E. (1988) *School Focused Staff Development. Guidelines for Policy Makers*, London, Falmer.
11 Drucker, P. (1989) in C. Morgan and V. Riches (eds) *Human Resource Management in Education*, Milton Keynes, Open University Press.
12 Dixon, N.F. (1994) *The Psychology of Military Incompetence*, London, Pimlico.
13 Argyris, C. and Schon, D. (1978) *Organisational Learning: A Theory of Action Perspective*, Reading, MA, Addison Wesley.
14 Hargreaves, D.H. (1998) 'The knowledge-creating school', paper delivered at the British Educational Research Association, Belfast, August.

2 HUNT THE UNICORN

1 Hampden-Turner, C. and Trompenaars, L. (1993) *The Seven Cultures of Capitalism*, New York, Doubleday, p. 44.
2 Borger, J.B. *et al.* (1984) 'Effective Schools: a quantitative synthesis of constructs', *Journal of Classroom Interaction* 20: 12–17.
3 Scheerens, J. and Bosker, R. (1997) *Foundational Studies in School Effectiveness*, International Congress for School Effectiveness and Improvement, London, Pergamon.
4 Sammons, P., Hillman J. and Mortimore, P. (1994) *Key Characteristics of Effective Schools*, London, OFSTED.
5 Rutter, M., Maughan, B., Mortimore, P. and Ouston, J. (1979) *Fifteen Thousand Hours: Secondary Schools and Their Effects on Children*, Cambridge, MA, Harvard University Press.

6 Mortimore, P., Sammons, P., Stoll, L., Lewis, D. and Ecob, R. (1988) *School Matters: The Junior Years*, Somerset, Open Books.

7 Scheerens, J. (1992) *Effective Schooling: Research, Theory and Practice*, London, Cassell.

8 Teddlie, C. and Stringfield, C. (1985) 'A Differential Analysis of Effectiveness in Middle and Lower Socio-economic Status Schools', *Journal of Classroom Interaction* 20, 2: 38–44.

9 Vermeulen, C.J. (1987) 'De effectiviteit van onderwijs bij zeventien rotterdamse stimuleringsscholen', *Pedagogische Studieen*, 64: 49–58.

10 Hampden-Turner, C. and Trompenaars, L. (1993) *The Seven Cultures of Capitalism*, New York, Doubleday, p. 38.

11 Sammons, P., Hillman, J. and Mortimore, P. (1994) *Key Characteristics of Effective Schools: A Review of School Effectiveness Research*, London, Office for Standards in Education.

12 Thomas, S., Pan, H. and Goldstein, H. (1994) *Report on the Analysis of 1992 Examination Results: AMA Project on Putting Examination Results in Context*, London, Association of Metropolitan Authorities.

13 Gillborn, D. and Gipps, C. (1996) *Recent Research on the Achievements of Ethnic Minority Pupils*, London University Institute of Education, OFSTED.

14 Hampden-Turner, C. and Trompenaars, L. (1993) *The Seven Cultures of Capitalism*, New York, Doubleday, p. 7.

15 Ibid., p. 20.

16 MacBeath, J. (ed.) (1998) *Effective School Leadership: Responding to Change*, London, Paul Chapman.

17 Willms, J.D. (1985) 'The Balance Thesis – Contextual Effects of Ability on Pupils' "O" grade examination results', *Oxford Review of Education* 11, 1: 33–41.

18 For example, Brookover, W.B., Beady, C., Flood, P. and Schwietzer, J. (1979) *School Social Systems and Student Achievement: Schools Can Make a Difference*, New York, Praeger.

19 Coleman, J. (1995) 'An inside-out approach to school improvement' paper delivered at Eighth Annual Congress for School Effectiveness and School Improvement, Leeuwarden, January.

20 Feuerstein, R., Rand, Y., Hoffman, M.A. and Miller, R. (1980) *Instrumental Enrichment: An Intervention Programme for Cognitive Modifiability*, Baltimore, University Park Press.

21 Mortimore, P. (1991) 'School Effectiveness Research: Which Way at the Crossroads?' *School Effectiveness and School Improvement*, 2, 3: 213–29.

22 MacBeath J. and Mortimore P. (1994) 'Improving school effectiveness: a Scottish approach', paper presented at British Educational Research Association, Oxford, September.

23 Steiner-Löffel, U. (1996) 'Pupils evaluate school culture: a photographic approach', paper presented at the European Educational Research Association, Seville, September.

24 Ibid., p. 9.

25 MacBeath, J. and Turner, M. (1991) *Learning out of School*, Scottish Education Department, Glasgow, Jordanhill College of Education.

26 MacBeath, J. (1998) 'Just Think About It', *Times Educational Supplement*, 10 April: 13.

27 Huberman, M. (1988) 'Teachers' careers and school improvement', *Journal of Curriculum Studies* 20, 2: 119–32.

28 OECD/CERI (1995) *Education at a Glance* (volume 3), Paris, Organisation for Economic Co-operation and Development.

29 Robinson, P. (1998) Parliamentary Brief, May: 59–60.

30 Kerr, C. (1991), 'Is Education Really all that Guilty?' *Education Week*, 7 February: 30.

31 Ibid.

32 Bracey, G.W. (1992) 'The Second Bracey Report on the Condition of Public Education', *Phi Delta Kappan* 74, 2: 104–17.

33 Ibid.

34 Goh Chok Tong (1997) 'Singapore', report given at the Seventh International Conference on Thinking Skills, Singapore, June.

35 National Commission on Education (1993) *Learning to Succeed*, London, Heinemann.

36 Desforges, C. (1995) *An Introduction to Teaching: Psychological Perspectives*, Oxford, Blackwell.

37 Medawar, P. (1998) 'A Note on "The Scientific Method"' in *The Sickening Mind, Brain, Behaviour, Immunity and Disease*, London, HarperCollins, p. 7.
38 See, for example, Lozanov, G. (1991) 'On Some Problems of the Anatomy, Physiology and Biochemistry of Cerebral Activities in the Global-artistic Approach in Modern Suggestopedagogic Training', *The Journal of the Society for Accelerative Learning and Teaching* 16, 2: 101–116; Gardner, H. (1983) *Frames of Mind*, New York, Basic Books; Gardner, H. (1993) *The Unschooled Mind*, London, Fontana; Gardner, H. (1997) *Leading Minds. An Anatomy of Leadership*, London, HarperCollins; and Sternberg, R.J. (1996) *Successful Intelligence: How Practical and Creative Intelligence Determine Success in Life*, New York, Simon & Schuster.

3 HOW THE FRAMEWORK WAS DEVELOPED

1 *References to pp. 29–31.*

Achilles, C., Nye, B.A., Zacharias, J.B. and Fulton, B.D. (1993) 'Creating Successful Schools for all Children: A Proven Step', *Journal of School Leadership* 3: 606–21.
Brookover W. *et al.* (1979) *School Social Systems and Student Achievement: Schools Can Make a Difference*, New York: Praeger.
Brophy, J.E. and Good, T.L. (1986) 'Teacher Behaviour and Student Achievement', in M. Wittrock (ed.) *Third Handbook of Research on Teaching*, New York, Macmillan.
Cuttance, P. (1986) *Effective Schooling: A Report to the Scottish Education Department*, Edinburgh, Centre for Educational Sociology, University of Edinburgh.
Cuttance, P. (1987) *Modelling Variation in the Effectiveness of Schooling*, Edinburgh, Centre for Educational Sociology, University of Edinburgh.
Cuttance, P., McPherson, A., Raffe, D. and Willms, D. (1988) 'Secondary school effectiveness', report to the Scottish Education Department, Centre for Educational Sociology, University of Edinburgh, August.
Epstein, J.L. (1992) 'School and Family Partnerships', *Encyclopedia of Educational Research*, sixth edition, M. Alkin (Ed.), New York, Macmillan.
Epstein, J. and Dauber, S.L. (1991) 'School Programs and Teacher Practices of Parent Involvement in Inner-city Elementray and Middle Schools' *The Elementary School Journal* 91, 3: 289–305.
Grisay, A. (1996) *Evoluation des acquis cognitifs et socio-affectifs des élèves au cours des années de college*, Liège, Universite de Liège.
Hargreaves, D.H. (1995) 'School Culture, School Effectiveness and School Improvement', *School Effectiveness and School Improvement* 6: 23–46.
Hill, P.W., Rowe, K.J. and Jones, T. (1995) *School Improvement Information Service. Version 1.1*, Melbourne, University of Melbourne, Centre for Applied Educational Research.
Lee, V., Bryk, S. and Smith, J. (1993) 'The Organisation of Effective Secondary Schools', in L. Darling-Hammond (ed.) *Review of Research in Education* 19: 171–226, American Educational Research Association, Washington, DC.
Lezotte (1989) 'Base School Improvement on What We Know about Effective Schools', *The American School Board Journal* 176, 8: 18–20.
Lightfoot, S.L. (1983) *The Good High School: Portraits of Character and Culture*, New York, Basic Books.
Lipitz, J. (1984) *Successful Schools for Young Adolescents*, New Brunswick, NJ, Transaction Books.
Little, J.W. (1988) 'Assessing the Prospects for Teacher Leadership', in A. Liebermann (ed.) *Building a Professional Culture in Schools*, New York, Teachers' College Press.
MacGilchrist, B., Mortimore, P., Savage, J. and Beresford C. (1995) *Planning Matters: The Impact of Development Planning in Primary Schools*, London, Paul Chapman Publishing.
Mortimore, P., Sammons, P., Stoll, L., Lewis, D. and Ecob, R. (1988) *School Matters: The Junior Years*, Somerset, Open Books.
Murphy, J. (1993) *Restructuring Schools*, London, Cassell.
Postlethwaite, T.N. and Ross, K.N. (1992) *Effective Schools in Reading: Implications for Educational Planners*, The Hague: IEA.

Purkey, S.C. and Smith, M.S. (1983), 'Effective Schools: A Review', *Elementary School Journal*, 83, 4: 427–52.

Rutter, M., Maughan, B., Mortimore, P. and Ouston, J. (1979) *Fifteen Thousand Hours: Secondary Schools and Their Effects on Children*, Cambridge, MA, Harvard University Press.

Sammons, P. (1993) 'Findings from school effectiveness research: some implications for improving the quality of schools', paper presented to seminar series Improving Education: The Issue is Quality, Birmingham University School of Education and Birmingham LEA and to be published in a volume of seminar papers by Cassell.

Sammons, P. (1994) 'Gender, Ethnic and Socio-economic Differences in Attainment and Progress: A Longitudinal Analysis of Student Achievement over 9 Years', *British Educational Research Journal* 21, 4: 465–85.

Scheerens, J. and Creemers, B.P.M. (1996) 'School Effectiveness in the Netherlands: The Modest Influence of a Research Programme' *School Effectiveness and School Improvement* 7: 181–95.

Slavin, R.E. (1989) *School and Classroom Organisation*, New Jersey, Erlbaum Hillsdale.

Slavin, R. (1995) 'Success for all: restructuring elementary schools', paper presented at the Eighth Annual Congress for School Effectiveness and Improvement, Leeuwarden, January.

Smith, D. and Tomlinson, S. (1989) *The School Effects: A Study of Multi-racial Comprehensives*, London, Policy Studies Institute.

Walberg, H.J. (1993) 'National data bases and public policy', paper presented at the American Educational Research Association, Atlanta, April.

Willms, J.D. (1985) 'The Balance Thesis – Contextual Effects of Ability on Pupils' "O" Grade Examination Results', *Oxford Review of Education* 11, 1: 33–41.

Other references, to Coleman (1982), Evertson (1980), Hedges (1994), Hersch (1981), Behling (1982), Squires (1983), Trisman (1976), Turner (1985) are contained in two comprehensive reviews of the literature by Jaap Scheerens (1992) *Effective Schooling*, London, Cassell, and J. Scheerens and R. Bosker (1997) *Foundational Studies in School Effectiveness*, London, Pergamon.

2 Mortimore *et al.* (1988), *op. cit.*

3 Grisay, *op. cit.*

4 McGaw, B., Banks, D. and Piper, K. (1991) *Effective Schools: Schools that Make a Difference*, Hawthorn, Victoria: Australian Council for Educational Research.

5 MacBeath, J./MVA (1989) *Talking about Schools*, Edinburgh, Scottish Education Department, p. 10.

4 EXPLORING THE THEMES

1 See, for example, Stoll, L. and Fink, D. (1996) *Changing our Schools*, Milton Keynes, Open University Press.

2 For example, Hargreaves, D. (1995) 'School Culture, School Effectiveness and School Improvement', *School Effectiveness and School Improvement*.

3 Achilles, C. *et al.*, *op. cit.*

4 Campbell, R.J. and Neill, S.R. (1992) *Primary Teachers at Work*, London, Routledge.

5 Bennett, N. (1994) *Class Size in Primary Schools*, Exeter, University of Exeter.

6 Galton, M., Hargreaves, L. and Pell, A. (1996) *Class Size, Teaching and Pupil Achievement*, Leicester, Leicester University School of Education (Commissioned by NUT).

5 THE GOOD TEACHER

1 A classic text is J.S. Kounin (1970) *Discipline and Group Management in Classrooms*, New York, Holt, Rhinehart, Winston.

2 Coleman, P. and Collinge, J. (1995) 'An inside-out approach to school improvement', paper delivered at Eighth Annual Congress for School Effectiveness and School Improvement, Leeuwarden, January.

3 See, for example, J. Rudduck (1996) *School Improvement: What Can Pupils Tell Us?* London, David Fulton.

6 INSPECTION PRIORITIES

1 OFSTED (1995) *New Framework for School Inspection*, London, Standards and Effectiveness Unit, Department for Education.

7 WHAT HAPPENED NEXT?

1 Available from National Union of Teachers Headquarters, Hamilton House, Mabledon Place, London.
2 Barber, M. (1996) *The Learning Game: Arguments for an Education Revolution*, London, Victor Gollanz.
3 Office for Standards in Education (1998) *Evaluation Matters*, London, Standards and Effectiveness Unit, Department for Education and Industry.
4 H.M. Inspector of Schools, Audit Unit (1997) *How Good is Our School?*, Edinburgh, Scottish Office Education and Industry Department, HMSO.
5 Bradford Inspection, Support and Advisory Service.
6 Office for Standards in Education (1997) *Report on Asmall Primary School* (available on Internet site: Asmall Primary School), p. 102.

8 WHAT HAPPENS IN OTHER COUNTRIES?

1 Alvik, T. (1997) *School Self-evaluation: A Whole School Approach*, Dundee, CIDREE Collaborative Project, Scottish Consultative Council on the Curriculum.
2 Landelijk Aktie Komitee Scholieren (1995) *Checklist om een Gouden School to Worden*, Amsterdam, LAKS.
3 Ministerio de Educación y Cultura (1997) *Guía Para la Autoevaluación*, Madrid, Argentaria.
4 Bertelsmann Stiftung, *Innovative school systems in an International Comparison*, Volume *Documentations of the International Research*, Gütersloh, Bertelsmann Stiftung.
5 Jakobsen, L., MacBeath, J., Meuret, D. and Schratz, M. (1998) 'Evaluating quality in 101 schools', paper presented at the American Educational Research Association, San Diego, April.
6 http.//www.acts.tinet.ie/quality/
7 Nevo, D. (1995) *School-based Evaluation: A Dialogue for School Improvement*, Oxford, Pergamon.
8 Smith, W., Moos, L. and MacBeath, J. (1998) 'School Self-assessment: quality in the eye of the stakeholder', paper presented at the American Educational Research Association, San Diego, April.
9 Vidot, G. (1996) 'Assuring Quality: Balancing Accountability and Development', *Nexus* 2, 1.
10 Scottish Office Education Department (1992) *Using Ethos Indicators in Primary School Self-evaluation: Taking Account of the Views of Pupils, Parents and Teachers*, HM Inspectors of Schools.

9 A FRAMEWORK FOR SELF-EVALUATION

1 Huber, S.G. (1998) 'Dovetailing school effectiveness and school improvement', paper delivered at the International Congress for School Effectiveness and School Improvement, Manchester, January, p. 19.
2 Hackman, J.R. and Oldham, G. (1975) 'A New Strategy for Job Enrichment', *California Management Review* 17, 4: 57–71.
3 Ibid., p. 57.
4 Eisner, E. (1991) *The Enlightened Eye*, New York, Macmillan, p. 34.
5 Ibid.
6 Scheerens, J. and Bosker, R., *op. cit.*

12 SUMMARY AND RECOMMENDATIONS

1 Reynolds, D. and Cuttance, P. (1992) *School Effectiveness: Research, Policy and Practice*, London, Cassell.
2 For example, Huberman, M. and Miles, M. (1984) *Innovation Up Close: How School Improvement Works*, New York, Pergamon Press.
3 Ball, S.J. (1994) *Comprehensive Schooling Effectiveness and Control: An Analysis of Educational Discourses*, London, Centre for Educational Studies, King's College.

INDEX

ability 11–12
accountability 5–6
achievement recognition 55–6; indicators 34, 56, 146–7; previous studies 30
Achilles, C. 30
adaptability to change 51
Alvik, T. 90, 91, 92, 96
Anderson, Lindsay 4
appraisal systems 76–7
Argentina 95
Argyris, C. 7
Asmall Primary School 84–7
Australia 94–5
Austria 91
authorities 75–8, 82, 87–9, 154

Ball, S. 154
Bangs, John 88
Barber, Michael 72, 73
Barthes, R. 6
Behling 31
Bennett, N. 48
Blunkett, David 72
Blyton, Enid 4
Borger, J.B. 9
Bosker, R. 9, 112
Bracey, G. 18
Brookover, W. 30
Brophy, J.E. 30
Bryk, S. 31
bullying 4, 57

Canada 94
CIDREE 113
class size 47–8, 139
classroom climate 41–3; indicators 43, 134–5; previous studies 30
Coleman, J. 14, 29
Coleman, P. 59
collaboration 70
communications *see* organisation and communication

community 13–14
confidentiality 109
Conservative Party 71–2
Creemers, B.P.M. 30
criteria 23; establishing 111–12, 118–20; OFSTED 22, 29, 32, 64–70, 78, 80; *see also* indicators
critical friend 110–11, 112, 116–17, 119–21
critical incident analysis 143
curriculum 68–9
Cuttance, P. 31

data, qualitative and quantitative 112–13
Denmark 90, 99–103
Desforges, C. 19
diaries 141
differential effectiveness 11
discipline 37, 42, 62–3, 116
discrimination 54
Drucker, P. 7

education market 6
Edwardson, Roger 87–9
Epstein, J.L. 31
equal opportunities culture 52–3
equality 62, 69
equity 32–3, 52–5, 133; indicators 34, 54–5, 144–5; previous studies 31
ethnic groups 11–12
ethos indicators 131
European Commission: 'Evaluating Quality in School Education' 83, 92; 'Guide to School Self-evaluation' 113
evaluation: classification 96; criteria 23; forms of 90; internal and external 152, 153–4; international comparison 90–103; objective and subjective 73; political 5; purpose of 4–8, 16–17; three dimensions 2–3; *see also* self-evaluation
Evertson 30
expertise, hidden and available 113
extra-curricular activities 37–8

162